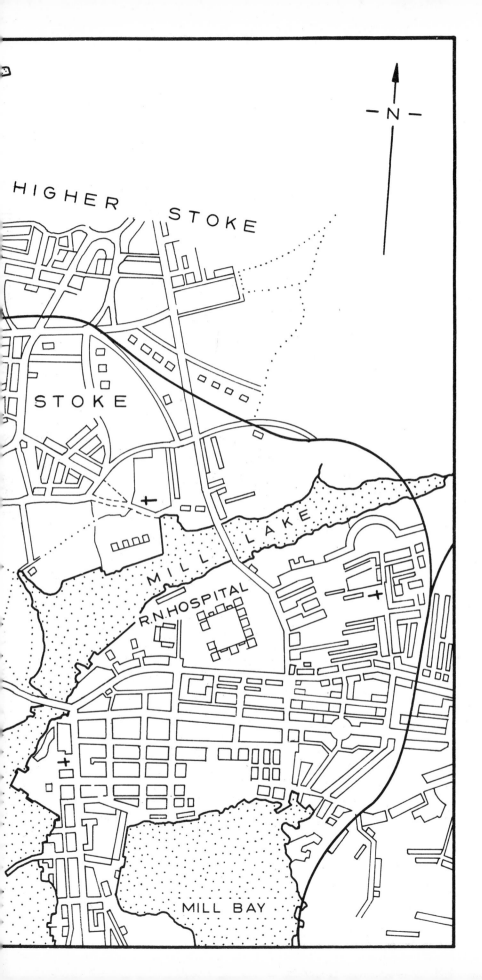

THE BOOK OF PLYMOUTH

FRONT COVER: Citadel Pool, Queen Anne's Battery, Plymouth.

St Andrew's Church and Guildhall. (LS)

THE BOOK OF PLYMOUTH

BY

JOHN GERRARD

BARRACUDA BOOKS LIMITED
BUCKINGHAM, ENGLAND
MCMLXXXII

PUBLISHED BY BARRACUDA BOOKS LIMITED
BUCKINGHAM, ENGLAND
AND PRINTED BY
HOLYWELL PRESS LIMITED
OXFORD, ENGLAND

BOUND BY
HAZELL, WATSON & VINEY LIMITED
AYLESBURY, BUCKS

JACKET PRINTED BY
CHENEY & SONS LIMITED
BANBURY, OXON

LITHOGRAPHY BY
BICESTER PHOTO LITHO LIMITED
BICESTER, ENGLAND

DISPLAY SET IN BASKERVILLE
AND TEXT SET IN 11/12pt BASKERVILLE BY
SOUTH BUCKS PHOTOSETTERS LIMITED
BEACONSFIELD, ENGLAND

© John Gerrard 1982

ISBN 0 86023 153 4

Contents

Acknowledgements

It would be impossible to produce a book of this nature without the considerable help of a great many people. Staff of the Devon County Library Service have given generously of their time and advice. My sincere thanks go to Miss A. J. Shute, County Librarian, for permission to reproduce most of the illustrations used in the book, Mr F. Clarke, at Library Headquarters in Exeter, Mr Elliot, the Chief Librarian at Plymouth and Mrs J. Bristow and staff of the Local History Section of Plymouth Library.

I am also pleased to acknowledge the cooperation of the Director, Mr J. Barber, and staff at the Plymouth City Museum and Art Gallery. Mr W. H. Scutt, Assistant Keeper of Archaeology and Local History, kindly let me photograph some of the local exhibits in that Museum.

Additional illustrations have been kindly provided by Chris Symons (CS) and Geoff Dowling (GD). The maps were drawn by Jean Dowling and the pen and ink drawings by Tim Groghan. Some of the photographic work was undertaken by Ron Swift and Geoff Dowling.

The majority of the illustrations have been provided by the Library Service (LS) but some are of Museum exhibits (MS) and of the *Western Morning News* (WMN). These are acknowledged in the book.

Sweet Plym

How oft by Fancy led,
Sweet Plym, at morn or eve, I stray with thee:
But chief at shadowy eve I linger where
The ocean weds thee, and delighted view,
Proud rising o'er the vast Atlantic surge,
Thine own, — thy Plymouth, — nurse of heroes — her
'Who bears thy noble name.'

The azure Sound,
The reservoir of rivers. Silvery bays
Are seen where commerce lifts the peaceful sail,
Or where the war-barks rise; the indented coast
Frowns with wave-breasting rocks, nor does the eye
Forget the proud display of bustling towns,
And busy arsenals, and cliffs high-crowned
With pealing batteries and flags that wave
In the fresh ocean gale.

Carrington

Foreword

By Cllr. R. C. Scott, the Lord Mayor of Plymouth

At a time when the world seems to be getting smaller and more disturbing, as man reaches out to conquer space, more and more people are finding comfort and satisfaction in the past. They attempt to discover just how their forefathers coped with the tremendous problems of *their* day with only a fraction of the aids we have at our disposal in this technology-minded twentieth century.

This interest in the past is understandably even greater at local level, as men and women pore over old records to research their ancestry, to see what part their fathers played in events of yesterday, how their town or city developed, what outstanding figures helped shape it and what buildings once stood on land now covered by shopping complexes and office and factory buildings.

The past has never failed to interest me but it was not until I came to Plymouth in the early 1950 s that I realised just how prominent a part the City has played in the history of the British people.

It is all described in colourful prose and with great detail in this splendid *Book of Plymouth*. It provides a great deal of new information and is supported by more than 200 illustrations of old and new Plymouth.

All who love Plymouth will not fail to detect the author's affection for the city and he manages not only to hold our interest throughout, but to convey to the reader his pride in the City where he was born and raised.

The author takes us back to the Bronze Age when Plymouth was a settlement of sorts, right through the Middle Ages to May of this year, and devotes three whole chapters to events in the City during this century.

This is, of course, but one of many splendid books about Plymouth, several of which have been published since the City began to re-build after the war-time blitzes, but the author deserves congratulations on producing such a scholarly and entertaining work in approximately only 40,000 words and Barracuda Books deserve praise also for yet another excellent addition to their already popular series of town (and city) histories.

R. C. Scott

The City Arms

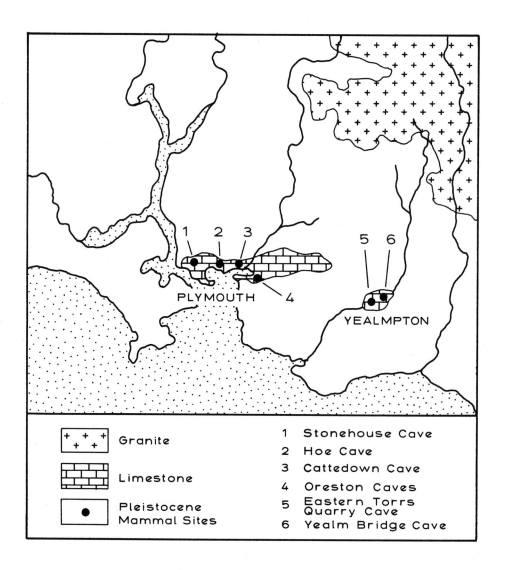

+ + +	Granite	1	Stonehouse Cave
		2	Hoe Cave
	Limestone	3	Cattedown Cave
		4	Oreston Caves
●	Pleistocene Mammal Sites	5	Eastern Torrs Quarry Cave
		6	Yealm Bridge Cave

Limestone caves in which traces of early man and mammals have been found.

Foundations

The intricate pattern of hill and valley, river and estuary, characteristic of the site of Plymouth, has had a profound influence on events in the city's past. The pattern was created when the ice masses of the last glacial period melted, about 10,000 years ago, raising the sea-level to its present height. The flat-topped plateau of the Hoe, a former marine beach, indicates that even higher sea-levels have existed.

Shelter from harsh climates was a major requisite for the survival of early man and animals. This was provided by the numerous caves that exist in the outcrops of Devonian Limestone that occur in a band from Plymouth to Buckfastleigh and Torquay. Woolly mammoth, woolly rhinoceros, reindeer, bear and other animals found shelter in the caves at Stonehouse, Oreston, Mount Wise and Pomphlet as bones found during the late eighteenth and early nineteenth centuries testify. It was not until 1887 that the first evidence of people was positively identified. The remains were in the famous Cattedown Cave (excavated by R.N. Worth and Robert Burnard). Continued occupation of the area since the Ice Age is reflected in the flint arrow head found on the Hoe, a deer horn pick unearthed in excavations for Keyham Docks, and a kitchen midden, consisting of seashells, found at Mount Batten.

Relics of the Bronze Age are more numerous. This is not surprising, as the hut circles and pounds on Dartmoor suggest a sizeable local population then. The slopes of Dartmoor were probably more settled than the coastal areas, but trackways running inland from the coast must have existed, and one of the most important was probably the same route followed today by the Plymouth — Yelverton road. Many of the more substantial finds show the local settlement area was continuous from the Late Bronze Age (about 1,000 BC) to the end of the Roman Period. At Mount Batten, in 1882, a quarryman found five gold and eight silver coins. Subsequently other coins were found and dated to between 100 BC and AD 100. In an Iron Age cemetery (opened in 1864) between Fort Stamford and Mount Batten, the graves contained numerous articles in bronze, iron, earthenware and glass. Most significant were three bronze mirrors. Other finds were uncovered during the construction, between 1917 and 1920, of the RAF station at Mount Batten. These included a sickle, chisel, gouges and a knife of Late Bronze Age, and Iron Age brooches, pins and parts of bracelets. Much broken pottery was also found, ranging from Iron Age to coarse Romano-British (second to fourth centuries AD).

Evidence of Roman occupation is somewhat speculative. The Romans may have buried their dead on the southern shore of Stonehouse Creek, at Newport Street. In 1882, R. N. Worth reported that excavations for the construction of four cottages exposed a flat area paved with pebbles and slate slabs with, in one corner, a group of 14 or 15 small tombs of brick and stone, arranged in rows. Their construction, of thin tile bricks, and their size and arrangement suggested Roman origin. Other speculations include the possibility of a Roman settlement at Trematon, on a small creek of the River Lynher, and a signal station on the Plymouth side of the Tamar, near Kings Tamerton. Early fortifications, of uncertain age, were excavated in 1934 by E. N. Masson Phillips. Roman Way remains as a constant reminder of these possibilities, especially as the route from Plympton to Saltash, avoiding the creeks and inlets, must be an ancient one. Other evidence of a Roman presence includes glass pottery and coins found at Mount Batten and a small bronze statuette of the god Mercury, found in a garden at Hooe.

Then there are the huge figures of Gog and Magog which were carved in the turf of the Hoe. Legend suggests that Brutus the Trojan landed at Totnes and, despite the local race of giants, decided to settle. One day, as Brutus and his friends held a festival, the giants attacked. Eventually all the giants were killed, except Goemagot. Corineus, one of the chiefs of the Trojan party, wrestled with Goemagot, took the giant upon his back, ran with him to a high rock and hurled him into the sea. This rock, now the Hoe, was called Geomagot's Leap and the fight was commemorated by carving the figures of Goemagot and Corineus in the turf. The truth is more prosaic and reflects pagan worship of Iron Age time. The existence of the figures is confirmed in Corporation records. As early as 1494, entries referred to their cutting and renewal.

Records of the Dark Ages are essentially myths and legends about the ancient tribe of the Dumnonni, although some valuable information was provided by missionaries from Ireland, Wales and France. St Budoc, an abbot and Bishop of Dol in Brittany, is remembered in St Budeaux. Legends claim that he sailed up the Tamar and landed in Tamerton Creek, near Budshead, but there is no proof that he ever visited the area, although his supporters may have done so.

Towards the end of the seventh century the Saxons were moving steadily westwards from their main centre in Wessex, pushing the remnants of the Dumnonni into Cornwall. The Tamar estuary then became the frontier of Wessex. In 705, King Geraint of Cornwall gave the bishop of the new diocese of Sherborne five hides of land at Maker. (A 'hide' or ploughland was about 120 acres.) Saxon government, land tenure and manorial rule were soon established and the county of Devon was divided into hundreds and the hundreds into tythings. (A hundred was a district of approximately a hundred families and the tything one of ten, but these distinctions soon became blurred.) Plymouth was originally in the hundred of Walkhampton *(Wachetona)*, but later in the hundred of Roborough. Weston Peverell and Compton Gifford were two of the ancient tythings that remained until relatively late. All was not peace and tranquillity during this period, when the Vikings were frequently a nuisance. An entry in the *Anglo-Saxon Chronicle* for 997 describes how a Danish force travelled up the Tamar to Lydford, burning and slaying as it went. However, by the time of the Domesday Survey (1086), the area was well settled, with manor houses and cottages in the clearings in the woods and beside the creeks.

The original manor of Sutton (Sudtone) was bounded on the south by the Sound, by Stonehouse on the west and extended north to the old Stoke Damerel Fleet, later known as Deadlake and filled in as Victoria Park. Coxside was its appropriate eastern boundary. It was surrounded by the manors of Stonehouse, Stoke (Stoches), Mutley (Modlei) and the two Lipsons. The King was the Lord of the Manor of Sutton, the Saxon Alwin held Stonehouse, Mutley and Efford and Brismar held Stoke. Stoke was to become Damerel in Norman times because of the overlord's name, Robert d'Albermarle. The ownership of Buckland *(Bocheland)* by the Saxon Heche (Old English *Ecca*) probably accounts for the unusual name Eggbuckland. The derivation of some of the other names is more straightforward. Efford *(Elforde)* was Eppeford, the ford passable at ebb tide.

The embryonic settlement gradually grew in stature as a market town and seaport and by the end of the reigns of the three Edwards (1377) Plymouth had an estimated population of 1,700, making it slightly larger than Exeter. It had also established extensive trading links with France and Spain. This increasing importance can be seen in the assembly, in the reign of Edward I (1227), of 325 ships; probably the first gathering of the national fleet. This fleet was bound for Guienne to demand the restoration of the King's rights and the event was so important that the

King himself came down, but was forced to reside at Plympton Priory because suitable accommodation was not available in Plymouth.

This serves to remind us that, until the end of the thirteenth century, Plympton was the more important settlement. A monastery existed at Plympton in Saxon times and it is stated in a deed of 904 that it came into the possession of the King, Edward the Elder. The present church of Plympton St Mary was built on the ruins of the old Priory. The Domesday Survey records that Plympton was the wealthiest manor of the district and included land in parts of Plymstock, Brixton and Shaugh. This is apparent justification for an old rhyme which runs:

When Plymouth was a fuzzy down

Plympton was a borough town.

The Earls of Devon had been given a market at Plympton Erle in 1194. Sutton did not receive its market until 1254, with the rights going to the Prior of Plympton. This market took place on Thursdays and increased considerably the local influence of the growing town, with traders coming in from the countryside.

It is interesting to speculate on the origin of the name, Plymouth. Pre-Domesday spellings of Plympton are *Plymenton* and *Plimton*. The Domesday spelling is *Plintona* but by the thirteenth century had become Plympton. R. N. Worth believed that *Plintona* was derived from *Pen-lyn-tun*, the tun at the head of the lake, the lake being the Laira or Lairy estuary. It is probable that the river took its name from Plympton and not *vice versa*. Eventually Plymouth superseded Sutton as the name of the settlement at the mouth of the Plym.

The early fortunes of Sutton lay in the hands of the Valletort family. Henry I gave the manors of Sutton, Maker and Kings Tamerton to Reginald of Valletort. The chief manor of the Valletorts then was Trematon, but the family built a residence to the west of the hill on which stood the Norman predecessor of St Andrew's Church. This was at the junction of the roads leading to Sourpole (Millbay) and Stonehouse — an advantageous site, indicated in deeds dated 1370 and 1373 among the documents of the Earl of Mount Edgcumbe. The highway to Stonehouse ran along what were Bedford, Frankfort and King Streets to Fore Street, Stonehouse whence it turned south to the ferry at Devils Point. This ferry linked Sutton and the Valletorts to the manor houses and growing settlements on the Cornish side of the Tamar. This mansion site seems to represent the start of the old Plymouth. Eventually the original Sutton gave way to three centres of growth: Sutton Valletort, Sutton Prior and Sutton Ralf or Raf. Sutton Valletort lay on the north, Sutton Prior was the centre of the growing town and Sutton Raf to the east. The speed of development of the three can be gauged by the way they were described in 1440. Sutton Prior was described as a town, Sutton Valletort as a hamlet and Sutton Raf, a tithing.

This period also saw the rise of many religious houses. The first definite record of a vicar is given in Bishop Bronescombe's register, where William de la Stane is said to have been appointed to the vicarage of Sutton in 1264. Outlying chapels, under the care of St Andrew's, existed at St Budeaux, Pennycross and Stonehouse. A chapel was established on Drake's Island, first dedicated to St Michael then to St Nicholas, before it was destroyed during fortification in 1548.

In the early fourteenth century, friars moved into the area. There is no extant written record of the Black Friars, although the name is firmly established in Black Friars Lane and Black Friars House in Southside Street. The Black Friars' name appears on Don's map of 1762. After the dissolution of the monastery Black Friars House became a debtors' prison, then a meeting house for nonconformists under Nicholas Sherwill. In the late seventeenth century it had a congregation of Huguenot refugees and is now the gin distillery. The Grey Friars (Franciscans) began in Woolster Street and the White Carmelite Friars near Friary Station. After the Dissolution, the buildings of the White Friars came into the possession of the Sparke family, who lived there until 1714. The fine gate at the entrance, with the arms of Jonathan Sparke and his wife carved on the keystone, survived until the early nineteenth century.

The relatively rapid growth of the settlements led to numerous disputes between the various religious establishments and between the Valletort family and the Priors of Plympton. One famous conflict occurred in 1281 when John Valletort claimed that he was the Lord of the Manor of Sutton while the Prior claimed he owned the 'ville' of Sutton. The official enquiry at Exeter decided that the Prior's authority was limited to the built-up area, the Valletorts were Lords of the rest of Sutton and the harbour belonged to the King. At around the same time Plympton was losing trade to Plymouth, primarily as a result of the silting up of the Laira estuary, due to tinning activities on Dartmoor and increased sediment carried by the rivers. The increasing size of boats using the harbour also favoured Plymouth. Plymouth was boosted by the comings and goings of the Hundred Years War as the starting point for many expeditions, and played a major part in the provision of men and ships. Additionally, Plymouth and Dover, by an Act of Richard II (1390), were designated the only ports from which pilgrims could sail.

Plymouth, then as later, suffered because of the wars, especially from attacks by the French. A number of these occurred late in the 13th century, but the most famous attack took place on 1 August 1403, when 30 ships carrying 1,200 men, led by Sieur du Chastel of St Malo, sailed into the Sound, up the Cattewater and landed a mile north of the town. The French force marched into the town from the direction of the White Friars buildings and began fighting near modern Exeter Street. The Bretons managed to penetrate the narrow streets before nightfall and spent the night in hand-to-hand fighting, pillaging, burning and killing. The area has been known ever since as Breton Side. Attempts to penetrate the Old Town were beaten off and they retreated to their ships and sailed away the following morning. This event suggested the need for better fortifications and in 1404 Henry IV ordered a wall to be built around the town. Fortifications at the entrance to Sutton Harbour were certainly strengthened to complete the castle Quadrate, with its four angled towers. Mercantile trade was established, and boosted by the Act of Incorporation which made Plymouth a free borough, with one mayor and one community, capable of owning land. It was the first Devon town to be so incorporated. The first petition of Parliament was in 1411 but it was not until 1439 that the petition gained Royal assent. The Act set out the boundaries of the Borough and named the first Mayor, William Keterigge. Its first half century was a difficult period, with continuing conflict with France and the Wars of the Roses, but the foundation had been laid for the great events and men that were to place Plymouth in the national limelight in the sixteenth century.

Neolithic stone axe found at Ernesettle. (MS)

14

LEFT: Tile from Plympton Priory. (MS) RIGHT: Bronze Roman statuette of the God Mercury found at Hooe. (MS)

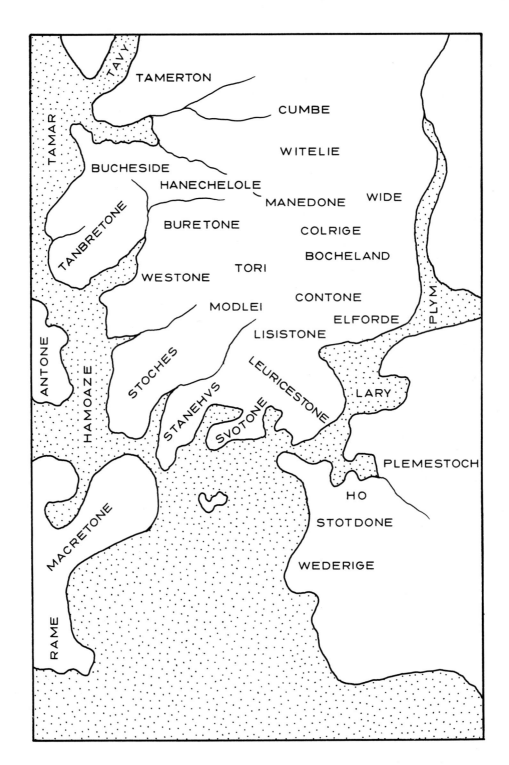

Domesday manors.

Tudor Men and Deeds

The story of Plymouth in the 16th century is one of men: the Hawkins, Drake, Gilbert, Grenville, Raleigh, many remembered as house names in Plymouth schools. It is a story of adventurers, sailors, privateers, colonizers and merchants. But it starts with the arrival of Catherine of Aragon at Plymouth, on 2 October 1501, on her journey to marry Prince Arthur, Henry VII's elder son. After her rough and hazardous sea voyage, she went to St Andrew's Church and gave thanks for her safety. Her welcome was a warm one and Corporation accounts show the extent of official hospitality. She spent a fortnight in the town, lodging in Palace Court house, which belonged to John Paynter, a merchant and several times Mayor of Plymouth.

The dissolution of the monasteries and the associated religious changes affected Plymouth considerably and their repercussions explain much of what happened during the next 100 years. The Bishop of Dover rode through the West Country in 1538, closing down the friaries and smaller religious houses. In Plymouth, he dealt first with the White Friars on 18 September and the Grey Friars the following day. The Grey Friars' establishment became the Mitre Inn, later removed to make way for the Exchange in 1813. The Woolster Street flats now occupy the site. The closure of these friaries caused little trouble or comment but when the Act of 1539 closed the larger institutions, greater conflict ensued. The destruction of Plympton Priory was extremely thorough and ruthless. It was used as a quarry, its stone going to build the village of Underwood. The Act severed the connection between Plymouth and the Priory, and the power to appoint the vicar of St Andrew's went to the Crown. In Queen Elizabeth's reign this power was given to the Corporation. As Plymouth and the Prior of Plympton had often been in dispute, the town welcomed the Reformation and this change.

The attitude of the town during the Rebellion which followed the establishment of the English Prayer Book, at the beginning of Edward VI's reign was hardly surprising — this era is known as Commocion Time. The Rebellion was triggered when, in April 1548, a Commissioner was stabbed to death by a priest while attempting to pull down images in Helston Church. The priest was hanged on 7 July and this led to a full-scale riot. A Cornish army gathered, and marched into Devon to besiege Exeter. On its way it attacked Trematon Castle and a portion moved on Plymouth. Large numbers of people rushed into the town from the surrounding countryside for protection. Among them were Edmond Drake, from Tavistock, an ardent Protestant, and his eight year-old son Francis. Little is known of the assault on the town but some of the town guns were set up on North Hill. The Cornishmen eventually drifted away to join the main party. After the Rebellion, Edmond Drake moved to the Medway and became Chaplain to the Fleet.

The link between the 15th and 16th centuries is provided by the Hawkins family, which originated in Kent. But a branch moved to Plymouth and a Hawkins held property in the town in 1480. It was William Hawkins, master of Henry VIII's Great Galley in 1513, who first brought the family to the nation's attention. He married a Trelawny family heiress and became one of the richest men in the area. He also made a lot of money exporting tin and wool and importing salt from France, wine from France, Portugal and Spain and fish from Newfoundland.

These were times when new continents were discovered: Columbus had crossed the Atlantic to North America in 1492. William Hawkins, in 1528, provided and commanded the *Paule of Plimmouth* on a year-long voyage which included trade with Brazil and the African Guinea Coast. Two more voyages to Brazil followed in quick succession and on his return in 1532 he was elected Mayor. He was Mayor again in 1538-9 and sat in Parliament for Plymouth in 1547 and 1553; the latter the year in which he died. In 1537 he had moved to a larger house on the east of Kinterbury Street, then a pleasant hillside facing Sutton Harbour. It was here that his two sons, William, the elder, and John were brought up. Both initially ran privateers in the English Channel, but John looked further afield and in 1562 organised a voyage to the West Indies. This was a slave-trading voyage in which negroes were taken from West Africa and sold to Spaniards in the Americas in return for pearls, sugar and hides. The voyage was extremely successful but some of the returning merchandise was seized by Philip of Spain. Animosity between Plymouth merchants and adventurers and Spain was kindled. The next voyage in 1564 was in the *Jesus of Lubeck*, with Royal approval. This was also the year Francis Drake returned to Plymouth from Kent with his own small ship. He took part in a little-known voyage to the West Indies financed by the Hawkins but his first major expedition was to the 'Bay of Mexico' in 1567 under the leadership of John Hawkins.

For this expedition Queen Elizabeth lent two ships; the *Jesus of Lubeck* and the *Minion* and the Hawkins family provided three of its own. Drake commanded his own small ship, the *Judith*, of 50 tons. After many skirmishes, the group were trapped at San Juan de Ulloa, the Mexican port of Vera Cruz. During the fighting the *Jesus of Lubeck* was destroyed, the *Swallow* sunk and the *Angel* abandoned. All that was left were the *Minion*, *Judith* and a Portuguese ship whose French captain had joined the expedition. These ships were too small to take off all the men and one hundred had to be left in Florida to be picked up later. The *Judith* returned on 20 January 1569 and on the 25th John Hawkins anchored in Mounts Bay unable to get any further without stores. These were sent by road and a few days later the *Minion* entered Plymouth.

The period leading to the Armada was one of conflict with Spain. William Hawkins had made improvements to the defences of the town and built a quay under the Castle barbican. Meanwhile Drake had married Mary Newman at St Budeaux Church on 6 July 1569. During the next few years Drake made a number of secretive voyages to the West Indies and Spanish Main. It transpired that these journeys were preparations for a major expedition, which left on 24 May 1572 with the ships *Pasha* and *Swan*. Drake's brothers, John and Joseph, sailed with him. The exploits of Drake on that voyage are well known. The crews were the first Englishmen to see the Pacific Ocean across the isthmus of Panama and, after many skirmishes, ambushed an captured a Spanish gold train in South America. This success was diminished by the deaths of his brothers, one of the fever and the other in action. Drake's return to Plymouth, on 9 August 1573, was greeted locally with wild celebration. Although secretly pleased, Elizabeth witheld official recognition because of the delicate relationship with Spain.

During the next few years Drake planned the expedition that was to lead to his circumnavigation of the globe. The ships he collected in the Cattewater were the *Pelican*, renamed *Golden Hind* (120 tons), *Elizabeth* (80 tons), *Marygold* (30 tons), *Swan* (50 tons) and the *Benedict*, a pinnace of 15 tons. (Pinnaces were often stored in the larger ships.) This group of ships sailed on 15 November 1577, but a gale forced them back into port for repairs and they did not finally sail until 13 December. They were reputedly heading for Alexandria but this was a feint. Drake passed through the Magellan Strait, up the west coast of both South and North America and decided, when the North West Passage did not materialise, to return via the

Pacific and Indian Oceans and the Cape of Good Hope. He had lost all his ships except the now-named *Golden Hind*, one of his officers had deserted and he was forced to execute another for repeated insubordination. Drake returned to Plymouth at Michaelmas 1580 and, after meeting the Mayor on board and enquiring whether the Queen was still alive and on the throne, wrote letters to her and to his backers. The accumulated treasure was stowed temporarily in Plymouth Castle. It was some time before the Queen, again because of relations with Philip of Spain, was able to acknowledge Drake and welcome him in triumph, with his prizes, to London.

Several major expeditions left Plymouth in the years up to 1588, two led by Humphry Gilbert. His first voyage was in 1578 and one of his ships was commanded by his half-brother, Walter Raleigh. This first voyage was a disaster. Fierce gales on 23 September forced the ships to return to Plymouth and start again two months later. This time a Spanish fleet caught and dispersed them off Cape Verde. Gilbert made one more attempt in 1583 and reached Newfoundland, which he claimed for the Queen, but on his way home his ships were overwhelmed by a storm near the Azores. Other expeditions followed: William Hawkins to the West Indies in 1582, Sir Richard Grenville to Virginia with the first of Raleigh's settlers in 1585 while Drake continuously harrassed Spanish ships from the Canaries to the West Indies. The ships for all these expeditions were provisioned and fitted-out in Plymouth and the town grew in prosperity.

The story of the Spanish Armada in 1588 has been told a hundredfold. During the early part of that year the Sound and Cattewater were thronged with naval ships, and crowds of volunteers streamed to the town to man them. The fleet put to sea several times to try to destroy the Spanish Fleet in their own waters, but each time the weather intervened. News came, on 19 July, that the Armada had been sighted off the Lizard. Whether Drake was playing bowls at the time is uncertain but it is highly unlikely that he would risk losing the Armada in order to finish the game, especially as it would take some time to get the ships and men in order. The manoeuvre that was to bring victory entailed sailing as far west and windward of the Spanish Fleet as was possible. Then Drake, with his smaller ships, ranged up and down the Spanish line giving it little chance to fight back. The battle raged at close quarters and the Spanish guns, on the high-built galleons, could not be depressed sufficiently to bring the English ships in range. The battle moved across the Channel to the French coast near Calais with the Spanish ships in considerable disarray. Lord Howard, the Lord High Admiral, had taken time during the battle to call Hawkins on board the *Ark Royal* and had knighted him, along with Frobisher. The Spanish Fleet was eventually routed and chased round the north of Scotland, pursued by Lord Howard, Drake and Hawkins.

Life in Plymouth then has been described by Bracken (1931). The chief streets were clustered around Sutton Pool but were spreading gradually towards Old Town. The streets would have been occupied by houses such as the 'Island House' and 32 New Street. The overhanging upper storeys, with diamond latticed windows, supported by carved corbels, would have made the streets dark but did offer some protection against the weather. The larger houses would have had broad staircases but many would have possessed pole staircases made of an old ship's mast, with the steps wound in a spiral around it. Many of the houses would have had gardens, as surprisingly many still do today in the Barbican area. These were the type of houses in which merchants and sea-captains lived. Drake lived at the top of Looe Street and the Hawkins in Kinterbury and Woolster Streets. Apprentices would have lived in tenements at the back of the merchants' houses while fishermen and poorer people lived in smaller houses, perhaps nearer the quay.

Maps of the time, especially Spry's Elizabethan leat map, show the principal roads. There were two routes to Stonehouse, one via the present Citadel Road route and the other from Frankfort Gate along Stonehouse Lane, avoiding the marshes on the south. To reach Stoke the road crossed Stoke Damerel Fleet at Sir Piers Edgcumbe's Mill Bridge, built in 1525. The major route north led to Maudlyn *(Mutley)* and on to Roborough. The route east had to cross the rivers Plym and Torry by ford and then wind its way through Plympton Marshes. To reach the other side of the Cattewater, a road led to Harstone *(Oreston)* Passage and a ferry. Scattered around the town were the large mansions of the rich and nobility. Sir Thomas Wise lived at Keyham, the Trelawny's at Ham and the Gorges had a house at Kinterbury. Efford Hall, Leigham House and Old Newnham (the Strodes) also existed at this time. The Harris family were living at Radford; Christopher Harris was a great friend of Drake and MP for Plymouth in 1583. The Parkers, living at Boringdon, were a new family from North Devon which later moved to Saltram. Warleigh was occupied by the Copplestones. The Copplestone oak tree, outside Tamerton Foliot church, is where the head of the family is supposed to have murdered his godson.

Most occupations were concerned with the sea, ships and shipping. Ships were built along the shores of the Cattewater and a number of rope walks existed. Wine was a major import, along with cloth, linen, iron ore etc. The Corporation strictly controlled all trade and commerce and levied what taxes it could. Prices were fixed and weights and measures checked repeatedly. The mills, pound and market paid special dues and the taverns had to pay for wine and ale licences. Charges were also made on the tonnage of ships entering Sutton Pool and on the landing of cargo.

Social order was strictly enforced and innkeepers were instructed to evict men and women of ill-fame and to prevent riot. Official records illustrate some of these situations. The multiplication of beggars consequent on the dissolution of the monasteries and the suppression of doles was described as one of the great plagues of the time. There were many outbreaks of true plague, one when Drake returned from his journey of circumnavigation. The Hoe was used frequently for hanging. In 1578 a man named Clerk was hanged and records show that it cost 11s 2d; 7s 6d for the gallows, 4d for carrying the ladder and 3s 4d for the the hangman. The town was harsh on undesirables, the ducking pool in the harbour in frequent use. Many undesirables were 'dumped' over the town boundary into Stonehouse, Stoke and Compton. Undesirable females chiefly went to Compton. An entry for 1602-03 states that 10s was paid to a certain Wrambie and his wife to keep them out of town.

After the defeat of the Armada, Drake embarked on his scheme to provide Plymouth with a water supply. He had bought Buckland Abbey from Sir Richard Grenville in 1588. The scheme, to take water by a leat from the River Meavy, was begun in December 1590 and completed in the following April. He received £200 from the Corporation and £100 to compensate landlords through whose property the leat ran. The Corporation held a survey of the water when it first arrived, a custom which is still maintained by way of the Fishing Feast.

Ten major expeditions left Plymouth between 1589 and 1595. In 1589 Drake sailed to Portugal to conquer the country but failed, and John Chudley sailed for the South Seas. John White took five ships with supplies for Raleigh's colonists in Virginia in 1580 and Sir John Hawkins and Sir Martin Frobisher sailed to Spain and the Azores. Expeditions in 1591 were unlucky. Sir Richard Grenville sailed for the Azores in the *Revenge* and perished in action against the Spanish fleet, while Cavendish took six ships to the Pacific but failed to navigate the Straits of Magellan and perished in the South Atlantic. In 1593 Richard Hawkins, in the *Dainty*, was captured by the Spanish in the Pacific Ocean and in 1595 Raleigh sailed on his first voyage to Guiana.

One of the last voyages of the 16th century was that led by Hawkins and Drake in 1595. Twenty seven ships assembled in the Cattewater and sailed on 28 August to attack Spanish America and invade Panama. This was an ill-fated expedition and Drake and Hawkins died within two months of each other in the Gulf of Mexico, and were buried at sea.

The era ended with the sad demise of Raleigh and the despicable behaviour of James I. Sir Walter Raleigh was put on trial on a false charge of treason and sentenced to be hanged. Instead of executing him, James had him sent to the Tower of London where he was held for thirteen years. He was only released on condition that he undertook a second voyage to Guina and brought back gold. Raleigh managed to scrape together seven ships and enough men, admittedly ill-prepared, to man them, but the voyage proved a disaster. Raleigh lost his son, most of his men and ships and alone in his ship named *Destiny* he returned to Plymouth on 21 June 1618. As Raleigh and his wife set out for London they were met by Raleigh's cousin, Sir Lewis Stukely, who was acting for the King. He had orders to arrest him and seize his ships. While the *Destiny* was being stripped of everything valuable, Raleigh stayed at Plymouth in a form of open arrest. That he did not try to escape says a lot for his integrity but it cost him his life, as he was taken eventually to London and beheaded. It is unfortunate that an era so packed with the deeds of heroic men should end in such a manner.

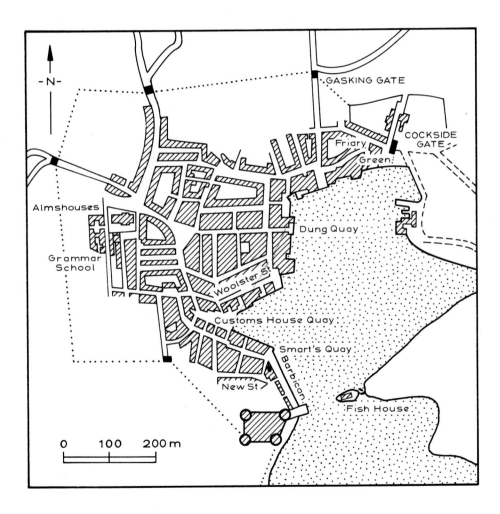

Extent of the town in the late 16th century (from a variety of sources).

ABOVE LEFT: Firestone Bay Tower, part of the defences dating from the time of Henry VIII. RIGHT: Part of Old Plymouth Castle, Lambhay Street. (LS) BELOW LEFT: Prysten House Porch. (LS) RIGHT: Prysten House, late 15th century attachment to St Andrew's Church. (LS)

22

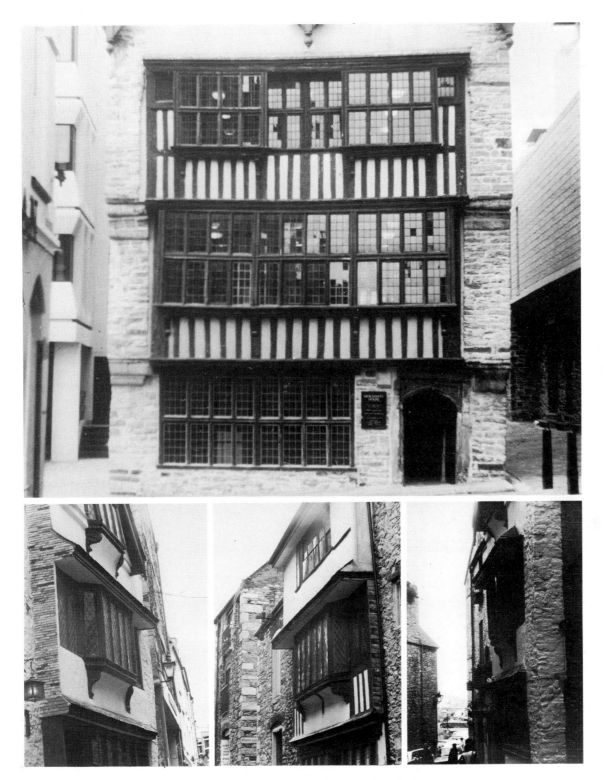

ABOVE: Merchant's House, now a local museum. BELOW: Elizabethan houses in New Street.

ABOVE: Drake's statue on the Hoe and plaque at foot of Drake's statue. BELOW: Armada memorial, the Hoe.

Town Under Siege

The first half of the 17th century was a momentous one in the history of Plymouth, with the departure of the Pilgrim Fathers and the Civil War. The impetus of trade and exploration of the Elizabethan and later years was consolidated by the colonizing of North America. Plymouth, along with Dartmouth, was heavily involved in the Newfoundland fishery trade, with Plymouth having 60 ships in the trade in 1631, involving about 2,400 seamen. The ships sailed to Newfoundland in the spring, erected wooden platforms on the shore where the fish were treated, and returned in August with their catches. Some of these ships, instead of returning direct to Plymouth, went first to Spanish and Mediterranean ports, selling their fish and buying local goods before returning. Imports included wine, salt, fruit, sugar, iron ore, paper and linen. Trade with Baltic ports also flourished. Exports from Plymouth were as varied, and included various metals and woollen goods. Most of Dartmoor's tin went through Plymouth as did some West Country lead. The two lowest of the six mills built by Drake beside his leat had changed from corn to fulling mills, where woollen cloth was cleaned and shrunk. These mills were situated where Cornwall Street crosses Armada Way.

The main overseas developments occurred in North America. The early Newfoundland fishermen had explored part of the coast southwards, Raleigh had tried settling Virginia and in 1602 Bartholomew Gosnold had built a fort at Martha's Vineyard, near Cape Cod. The involvement of Plymouth began with George Weymouth's return, in 1605, from explorations in New England. He gave gifts, including three Indians, to Gorges, then Governor of Plymouth. Gorges then joined with Chief Justice Popham, Raleigh Gilbert and William Parker to form the Plymouth Company of Virginia. They were granted a charter from the King, giving them all America between 41 and 45 degrees north (approximately New England).

An early attempt to found a colony failed and efforts were concentrated on setting up trading posts to buy furs from the Indians. Profits were substantial and in 1620 a new charter was sought for all trading, fishing and settlement rights from 40 to 48 degrees north, both on the Atlantic and Pacific shores. The Plymouth Company obtained its new charter and between 1621 and 1635 a number of land grants in New England were made by the Council of Plymouth. Plymouth men played a prominent part in the work of actual settlement.

The response of Plymouth to the Pilgrim Fathers and the stance of the town in the Civil War were connected threads in the collective feelings of Plymothians. Plymouth had always been sympathetic to nonconformists and its loyalty to the Crown was eroded by a succession of events in the first half of the 17th century. Elizabeth's attitude to religion had been one of uniformity; all subjects should conform to the State Church. Attempts by Roman Catholics or Puritans to organise communion in opposition to the Anglican Church were suppressed. The accession of James I did little to alter the situation. A number of active centres of separatist thought existed, one of the most prominent being in Lincolnshire where, for a number of years, John Robinson and John Smith had led dissenters in worship. When the risk of assembly became too great they moved to Amsterdam, then a haven for exiles, and later to Leyden.

Leyden also became insecure and in 1617 permission was sought for them and their followers to settle in Virginia. The patent to do so was finally received from the London Company in 1619 and the small group of pilgrims obtained two vessels, the *Speedwell* (60 tons) and the *Mayflower* (180 tons). *Mayflower* set sail from Delftshaven and on 19 July 1620 reached Southampton. The *Speedwell* followed a week later. They left Southampton on 5 August but the *Speedwell* was leaking badly and had to put into Dartmouth for repairs. *Speedwell* was still unseaworthy and the group put into Plymouth. It was decided that the *Speedwell* was unsuitable for the long Atlantic crossing and it was forced to return to London, but on 6 September 1620 the *Mayflower*, with 102 pilgrims on board, sailed from Plymouth. The names of some of these pilgrims are remembered on a plaque on the wall of the Island House on the Barbican, and the point presently nearest to their point of departure by the Mayflower Steps. They reached Cape Cod on 9 November and, after a first winter during which half of the group died of disease and starvation, established a permanent settlement. It seems clear that during their stay in Plymouth the pilgrims were well received.

The events during the next twenty years led to further alienation between town and Crown. Charles I was in urgent need of funds and in 1625 planned an expedition against Cadiz. Ninety ships were assembled in the Sound and 10,000 soldiers paraded on the Hoe. The King, Queen and the entire Court came to Plymouth and reviewed the army on Roborough Down. A prominent Plymouth dignitary, Sir James Bagge, was charged with fitting out the fleet. Bagge, who had been Mayor in 1595 and 1606 and Member of Parliament in 1601-03, was a friend of the Duke of Buckingham, confidant of the King. This was presumably how Bagge got the contract in the first place. The expedition proved a disastrous failure. The fleet was ill-equipped and the men ill-fed before they left. The army returned sick and sore and it was clear that Bagge had skimped on provisions and lined his own pockets.

Similar expeditions against France were made to Rochelle and Ile de Rhè, but each time the fleet and army limped back to Plymouth. The men were usually starving and disease ridden and rampaged through the local countryside, pillaging and spreading disease. It is understandable that the town resented this and blamed the King.

The town also quarrelled with the Crown over the appointment of the vicars of St Andrew's Church. Elizabeth had given authority to appoint the vicars of St Andrew's to the Mayor and Corporation, on condition that they found fit persons to serve the church and maintained a free Grammar School. The appointment of a vicar in 1634 caused a number of problems. The Corporation's first choice, Alexander Grosse, was rejected, as was the second choice, Thomas Ford. The King then instituted Dr Aaron Wilson, who held the living for ten years, during which time he quarelled continuously with the town. The town was so unhappy with this that in 1634 it petitioned for another church in which the ministry would be more in keeping with the Protestant cause. This was granted in 1640, when Parliament passed the Act delineating the new parish church. Charles' Church had risen to roof level, when the Siege of Plymouth started in 1643. It is suggested that a canvas roof was erected and the first service held in 1643 by the Presbyterian chaplain to the garrison. To emphasise the puritan ethic a door was opened in the east wall. As soon as the war had started, the town imprisoned Dr Wilson and sent him to Portsmouth. On his death the King named Bedford as vicar but Plymouth sent him away and appointed its own man, George Hughes.

The Civil War began in 1642, when King Charles raised his banner at Nottingham. This event initiated a momentous phase in the history of Plymouth, a phase still remembered in place names such as Mount Gould and Mount Batten. Mount Batten took its name from Captain Batten who was in charge of the defences there. Plymouth, in contrast to the West of England in general and Cornwall in particular, opted for Parliament. When Charles raised his banner, Plymouth Fort and Drake's Island were without a commander, as the King had appointed the then Governor of Plymouth, Sir Jacob Astley, as his major-general of foot. Thus, Thomas Ceely, the Mayor, took charge of fort and town until Parliament sent Colonel Ruthven to command the Plymouth garrison.

The Royalist leader in the west, Sir Ralph Hopton, attacked the town at the end of 1642, cutting off the water supply in the process, but was successfully repelled. It was clear that a long drawn-out struggle was in prospect and, early in 1643, an order was made for the extension of the town defences. The siege was the first occasion on which the town needed adequate landward defences and there is considerable speculation as to whether Plymouth was ever enclosed by walls. Many early historians have inferred that town walls did exist but doubt has been cast by James Barber. In a booklet *New Light on Old Plymouth*, reprinted from the Proceedings of the Plymouth Athenaeum, he had marshalled a wealth of information to suggest that, although town gates existed, town walls did not. There were many occasions when the building of walls was suggested as a top priority, notably during the reign of Henry VIII, but no proof that the work was ever undertaken. Early views and maps show the Castle, Causeway and Hoe foreshore with many guns, but no walls. In May 1592, Elizabeth granted the proceeds of a duty on pilchards towards the defence of the town, but the amount raised was sufficient only for the building of the Fort on the Hoe, and for strengthening the Henry VIII fortifications on Drake's Island. At the time of the siege, there were apparently no town walls and the inner line of defences was built rapidly in response to the emergency, and was probably largely earthwork with perhaps a thin facing of stone. The town at the time was bounded by a line that stretched from Fisher's Nose, at the entrance to the Cattewater, along the North Quay of Sutton Harbour, Ebrington Street, Frankfort Gate and Westwell Street, then around to the Hoe and back to the sea.

The intricate topography around the town was put to good use in designing the outer line of defence. There was little to fear from the sea, and effort was concentrated on building a line of stockaded earthworks, with a ditch, across the high ground between the indented creeks of Laira and Pennycomequick. More substantial forts were built along this line at Lipson, Holywell, Maudlyn *(Mutley)*, Pennycomequick and New-work *(Eldad)*. Other, isolated forts were constructed at Cattedown, Prince Rock, Laira Point, Lipson Mill, Mount Gould, Stonehouse, Stamford and Haw Stert. At the same time soldiers were brought in by sea until the town held about 9,000 men.

Late in 1643 events moved rapidly. In August, Colonel John Digby followed Hopton as commander of the Royalist forces. Sir Alexander Carew was then in command of Drake's Island but he was suspected of communicating with the Royalists at Mount Edgcumbe. When a party was sent to arrest him, the garrision was already holding him prisoner. He was sent to London and executed for high treason. Colonel James Wardlaw was then appointed Commander-in-Chief, assisted by Colonel William Gould. In September, Prince Maurice marched on Plymouth with five regiments of horse and nine of foot. These he stationed at Plymstock, Tamerton, Mount Edgcumbe and Cawsand, making his headquarters at Widey Court. Fort Stamford, on the east side of the Cattewater, was attacked by the Royalists for 17 days, during which it changed hands several times before finally falling. Colonel Gould was injured during one of the skirmishes. The Royalist cannon at Stamford could now bombard the Hoe, but did no more harm than shooting the vane off the Hoe windmill, and possibly injuring a woman in the arm. But Royalist cannon at Oreston already controlled the entrance to Sutton Harbour and guns on Mount Edgcumbe dominated Stonehouse Creek. Millbay was then the only free harbour and the defences on Drake's Island were crucial to the survival of the town.

The loss of Fort Stamford strengthened the town's resolve, and its inhabitants were united in the one cause, the defence of Plymouth. Thus, when asked to surrender by Prince Maurice, they resolutely refused and drew up a solemn vow and covenant for the defence of the town. Part of this vow and covenant, ordered to be taken by all, states: 'In the presence of Almighty God I vow and protest that I will to the utmost of my power faithfully maintain and defend the town of Plymouth and Stonehouse, the fort and island, with all the outworks and fortifications to the same belonging, against all forces now raised against the said town, fort and island, . . .'. There were further promises not to collaborate with the enemy: '. . . nor will I by any way or means give or yield to the giving of any advise, counsel or intelligence, to the prejudice of the said town . . . nor will I accept any protection from the enemy. And this vow or protestation I make without any equivocation or mental reservation whatsoever . . . so help me God'.

In spite of this vow, as in any war, treason and treachery did exist and we have already seen how Sir Alexander Carew was executed for treason. Then, late in 1643, Ellis Carkeet, a malignant mariner, was arrested for trying to persuade one Roger Kneebone, chief gunner at Maudlyn Fort, to blow it up. On his arrest, two of his accomplices, Henry Pike and Moses Collins, fled to the enemy and almost changed the entire course of the war. Early on the morning of 3 December 1643, they guided a party of Cavaliers across Lipson Creek at low tide. Lipson Creek then extended as far as Alexandra Road. This party crept around to the Laira Point Fort but was repulsed. Meanwhile, Prince Maurice and the main party had advanced around Lipson Creek from Compton Village and were advancing down the narrow valley from Eggbuckland. The defenders at Lipson Fort were soon outnumbered and drew back to Freedom Fields. Eventually the town rallied and, with Colonel Gould leading the attack, the Royalists were forced to retreat. The retreat soon became a panic, especially as the tide had now filled Lipson Creek and many horsemen were drowned attempting to cross it.

A further repulsed attack at Maudlyn Fort on 20 December, which cost the Royalists dear, persuaded Prince Maurice to raise the seige, but the town had only temporary relief from attack as the blockade was still in force. Indeed the Prince's last deed was to give an order to the constables of Eggbuckland and St Budeaux to guard against the relief of Plymouth. They had to report 'that if any person . . . presume to have any commerce or dealing with any in the said town, or take or carry with him any horse, oxen, kine or sheep, or other provision for man or horse, into the said town of Plymouth, for the relief of the rebels there, every such person and persons shall be proceeded against, both in person and estate . . .'

The town was certainly feeling the effects of the blockade and the death rate had risen enormously. The registers for St Andrew's for December 1643, which would normally have shown about twenty deaths, indicated 132. A remarkable thing then happened, as thousands of pilchards or mullets swam into Sutton Harbour within the Barbican. These were gathered up in buckets and many were salted and laid in store against future deprivations.

Early in 1644, Gould replaced Wardlaw as Governor and on the Royalist side Digby, who had sustained a wound in the eye, was replaced by Sir Richard Grenville, grandson of the Elizabethan Grenville. Grenville angered at Gould's refusal to surrender, attacked the country houses of Parliamentarians, hanged villagers and illtreated prisoners. Gould died in spring 1644 and was replaced by Colonel Martin, who kept up a strong offensive against the Royalists, with repeated armed sorties.

In September, the King marched on Plymouth in person, camped at Roborough and demanded surrender by a summons from his court at Widey. His daily sorties on the southern slopes of Hartley Hill merely earned, for his encampment, the derisive name 'vapourings', still remembered in Vapron Hill. The King finally attacked in a pincer movement at Pennycomequick and Milbridge but was repulsed with great loss to his men. Next day King Charles and Prince Maurice rode away and Grenville was left in charge. The last major attack on the town occurred in January 1645, when Grenville led 6,000 men against the entire defensive line. Maudlyn Fort was taken and re-taken before the Royalists were chased back down the hill to Mutley Plain. The tide of the war was now changing and Grenville went off to the siege of Taunton. The Royalist cause was collapsing and Fairfax was advancing. On the day that Parliament captured Dartmouth, 18 January 1646, the last Royalist left the siege of Plymouth and on 23 March, Fairfax and Cromwell were welcomed into Plymouth.

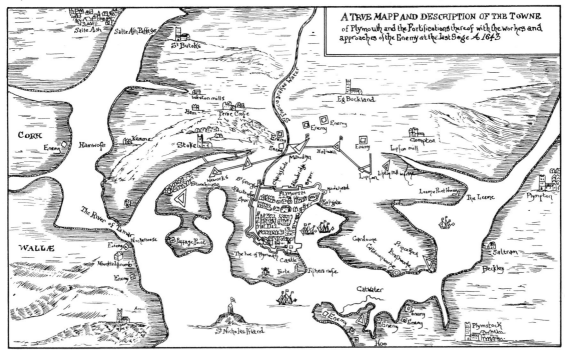

A TRVE MAPP AND DESCRIPTION OF THE TOWNE of Plymouth and the Fortifications thereof with the workes and approaches of the Enemy at the last Sege Aᵒ 1643

ABOVE: Plymouth at the time of the Civil War siege. LEFT: Model of Plymouth and Castle in 1620. (LS) RIGHT: King Charles I summons Plymouth to surrender during the Civil War. (LS)

Upon this spot, on Sunday December 3rd 1643, after hard fighting for several hours the Roundhead Garrison of Plymouth made their final rally, and routed the Cavalier Army which had surprised the Outworks and well nigh taken the town. For many years it was the custom to celebrate the anniversary of this victory long known as the "Sabbath-day fight," and recorded as the "Great Deliverance" of the protracted siege, successfully sustained by Troops and Townsfolk on behalf of the Parliament against the King under great hardships for more than three years.

PILGRIM FATHERS WHO SAILED FROM HERE
THE BARBICAN, PLYMOUTH, IN THE MAYFLOWER, 1620

MASTER WILL BRADFORD	FUSTIAN MAKER AUSTERF D. YORKS
JOHN CARVER	MERCHANT OF DONCASTER
MASTER EDWD WINSLOW	PRINTER OF DROITWICH
MASTER WILL BREWSTER	POSTMASTER, TUTOR, ETC
MASTER ISAAC ALLERTON	TAILOR OF LONDON
CAPT. MYLES STANDISH	SOLDIER OF CHORLEY LANCS
MASTER STEP'N HOPKINS	WOTTON UNDER EDGE GLOUCS TR.
MASTER CHRIS MARTIN	GREAT BURSTEAD ESSEX.
MASTER WILL MULLINS	SHOPKEEPER DORKING, SURREY
MASTER WILL WHITE	WOOL CARDER
MASTER RICH WARREN	MERCHANT OF LONDON.
EDWARD TILLEY	CLOTH MAKER OF LONDON
JOHN TILLEY	SILK WORKER OF LONDON.
PETER BROWNE	GREAT BURSTEAD ESSEX
FRANCIS EATON	CARPENTER OF BRISTOL
FRANCIS COOK	WOOL COMBER OF BLYTH
THOMAS ENGLISH	MARINER.
THOMAS TINKER	WOOD SAWYER
THOMAS ROGERS	MERCHANT.
JOHN RINGDALE	LONDON.
EDWARD FULLER	REDENHALL NORFOLK.
JOHN TURNER	MERCHANT.
JAMES CHILTON	TAILOR OF CANTERBURY.
JOHN CRACKSTON	COLCHESTER.
JOHN BILLINGTON	LONDON.
RICH BRITTERIDGE	GREAT BURSTEAD ESSEX.
RICHARD GARDINER	HARWICH ESSEX.
MOSES FLETCHER	SMITH OF SANDWICH.
JOHN ALDEN	COOPER OF HARWICH.
SAMUEL FULLER	SAIL MAKER.
JOHN GOODMAN	LINEN WEAVER.
DEGORY PRIEST	HATTER OF LONDON.
THOMAS WILLIAMS	YARMOUTH NORFOLK.
JOHN ALLERTON	MARINER.
JOHN HOOKE	SERVANT BOY.
RICHARD MORE	LONDON.
ROGER WILDER	MAN SERVANT.
WILLIAM LATHAM	SERVANT BOY.
JOHN HOWLAND	LONDON.
WILLIAM BUTTEN	AUSTERFIELD.
RICHARD CLARKE	EDMOND MARGESON
GILBERT WINSLOW	JASPER MORE.
EDWARD DOTEY	EDWARD LEISTER
JOHN LANGEMORE	ROBERT CARTER.
WILLIAM HOLBECK	EDWARD THOMPSON
GEORGE SOULE	ELIAS STORY.

On the 6th of September, 1620, in the Mayoralty of Thomas Fownes, after being "kindly entertained and courteously used by divers Friends there dwelling," the Pilgrim Fathers sailed from Plymouth in the Mayflower, in the Providence of God to settle in NEW PLYMOUTH, and to lay the foundation of the NEW ENGLAND STATES ~ The ancient Cawsey whence they embarked was destroyed not many Years afterwards, but the Site of their Embarkation is marked by the Stone bearing the name of the MAYFLOWER in the pavement of the adjacent Pier. This Tablet was erected in the Mayoralty of J. T. Bond 1891, to commemorate their Departure, and the visit to Plymouth in July of that Year of a number of their Descendants and Representatives.

LEFT: Memorial to the Battle of Freedom Fields, during the Siege of Plymouth. BELOW: Pilgrim Fathers and *Mayflower* remembered. RIGHT: Names of some of the Pilgrim Fathers on a wall of the Island House, Barbican.

18th Century Wars and Intrigues

Plymouth had survived the siege but had suffered severely in the process. The parish registers of St Andrew's provide one picture of what the Civil War cost Plymouth with more than 3,000 deaths registered during the siege. The town was also impoverished with food short and soldiers' wages unpaid. A tremendous amount of money had been borrowed from merchants, civic leaders and many others by the Committee of Defence. The surrounding countryside had also suffered and registers from parishes around Plymouth show the extent of the depredations by the Royalist forces. Most of the major houses had been damaged and gardens, orchards and cultivated land ravaged. Many of the local Royalist gentry were still restless and plans were made to capture Plymouth in the event of any rebellion. But the plans leaked out and the leader of the local Royalist group, Sir John Grenville, was gaoled. An abortive uprising did occur in March 1655, and the town responded by contructing hasty defences at North Hill.

Foreign trade had virtually ceased during the war and the Newfoundland fisheries had dwindled to virtually nothing. The American colonists, deprived of support and trade from England, had built up their own fishing fleets and had begun to trade among themselves and with the British colonies. The Navigation Act, passed in 1651, by forbidding foreigners to trade with the colonies, attempted to remedy this situation, but it only succeeded in starting the first Dutch war. This war, as did the succeeding one against Spain kept Plymouth busy again fitting and provisioning ships. The Old Castle became, for a time, a hospital, and a victualling establishment was built at Lambhay. A number of new buildings was erected during this immediate post-Civil War period. Charles Church was finally completed in 1657 and a new grammar school built within the Orphan's Aid in 1658. The Baptists survived the war as a viable congregation and in 1651 built themselves a meeting place in what was to become Bedford Street. Other religious groups developed and, in 1654, the Quakers arrived in the town, causing much hostility by protesting in the older churches. But many prominent families joined them and their numbers increased sufficiently to establish a Society of Friends. George Fox himself visited Plymouth in 1655.

When Cromwell died and his son Richard became Protector, there were many who feared that the forces of the left, Fifth Monarchy men, Quakers, Anabaptists etc., would take over the running of the country. Many of the older Parliamentary men preferred the idea of a king to rule by left-wing groups. One of these was William Morice, who had bought Werrington Park from Drake, and, in 1673, bought the Stoke Damerel estate from the Wise family. In 1660, he became Governor of Plymouth and was instrumental, along with other prominent men, in restoring Charles II to the throne. Plymouth welcomed Charles II but was clearly apprehensive about its future. As was feared by many, the next few years were difficult, with the Crown exacting a form of vengeance for the town's stance during the Civil War. Captain Westall, a Royalist spy, reported that in Plymouth Fifth Monarchy Men were encouraging Presbyterians in resisting Prayer Book rule. When the Royalist Parliament passed the Corporation Act, commissioners were sent down to evict the Mayor, William Allen, his Alderman and his Common Councillors and put in their place their own man, William Jennens. The 1662 Act of Uniformity was vigorously enacted and George Hughes, the vicar of St Andrew's, and his lecturer, Thomas Martyn, were seized a week before St Bartholomew's Day, 24 August, and taken to Drake's Island as State prisoners. They were replaced by king's men but Francis Porter of Charles Church kept his position.

Other frictions developed between the town and Charles II. Charles had a grandiose scheme for a Citadel on the Hoe, perhaps as much to overawe the town as its enemies. The King requisitioned the land on which it was built, as well as some adjoining land and houses. In order to build the Citadel, the existing fort was largely demolished, as was the chapel of St Katherine. Also, the figures of Corineus and Goemagot were destroyed. The military authorities had now laid claim to all the land on the Hoe. Building began in 1666, and the King paid several visits during construction. His brother, James accompanied him in 1671 and they stayed in the Citadel itself, while inspecting the Cattewater and the Hamoaze by day. In 1676 the King made a longer visit and enjoyed the hospitality of several local gentry. The Citadel was built, by Sir Bernard Gomme, on French principles with five bastions and two horn-works and was armed with 152 guns. The major architectural feature is the gateway, dated 1670, and attributed to Sir Thomas Fitz. The other remaining 17th century buildings are less impressive and are the guard house, governor's house, storehouse, chapel and officers' mess.

The town faced other provocations. The Crown was desperately short of money and there was persistent commandeering of both money and food. Press-gang activities were numerous. Charles then called for the surrender of the great Charter of Elizabeth and used Lord Chief Justice Jeffreys as his agent. This reduced the Corporation in power and numbers but Corporation property was secured by transferring it to trustees. The new Charter provided for a new Mayor, 12 new Aldermen; all to serve for life. James II, on his accession, surprisingly restored the Corporation to its original form and powers, but, in general, he rapidly alienated himself from his people. Thus, Plymouth rejoiced when William of Orange landed at Brixham and then welcomed his fleet into the Sound. Plymouth was the first town to declare William King, the Citadel was the first fortress handed over to him and a ship, in harbour at the time, was the first English warship to fly his flag. William's declaration was eventually read from the Bench of the Jacobean Guildhall by the Mayor.

Local industry during this period was largely concerned either with the sea and ships or with processing local commodities. Many naval contracts were obtained for ropes and cable yarn and the ropewalk at Teats Hill was kept busy. A weekly yarn market had existed for some time in the churchyard of St Andrew's church and was replaced, in 1653, by a proper yarn market built in Old Town. A new meat market was built in the middle of Old Town Street with a Leather Hall above it. Local accounts show that brewing was a common industry. The last quarter of the 17th and first quarter of the 18th century was a period when, although the commercial port of Plymouth was busy and still growing, it was losing ground to other ports. In 1716, Plymouth was ranked fourth in English ports behind London, Bristol and Exeter. But Bristol and Liverpool were building new docks and rapidly expanding their trade. Liverpool, with its favourable industrial hinterland, grew phenomenally and soon overtook Bristol. Plymouth was becoming something of a backwater, although foreign trade, especially to the West Indies and America, was growing. Local goods for export were limited to some woollens, lead, tin, copper and building stones. The major import was coal and there was a good coasting trade in foodstuffs and household requirements from London.

The numerous wars in the middle part of the 18th century, such as the War of the Austrian Succession 1741-8 and the Seven Years War, 1756-63, kept both Plymouth and Plymouth Dock (Devonport) busy. The three towns of Plymouth, Plymouth Dock and Stonehouse were growing to a sizeable combined settlement and overcrowding, lack of housing and insanitary conditions caused problems. There were attempts to make Plymouth a more attractive and healthy place to live. Rows of elm trees were planted in a number of places such as Millbay, Pennycomequick, Frankfort Gate and the Hoe. Many streets were paved and drains installed or improved. Rails and gates were erected on the Hoe but, with the expansion of the town, the town gates disappeared. Friary Gate was demolished in 1763.

George III made many visits to Plymouth and Plymouth dock, often with his sons the Prince of Wales, Duke of York and Duke of Clarence. On one occasion the King was accompanied by the Queen and the Princesses Royal, Augusta and Elizabeth. The Royal coaches were each drawn by six horses and the party stayed with Lord Boringdon at Saltram. The King reviewed the fleet and visited the Dockyard, Citadel and Victualling Office and social visits were made to the Earl of Mount Edgcumbe and to Sir Manasseh Lope's estate at Maristow. The King's sons were honoured by Plymouth. The Duke of York was made Lord High Steward in 1762 and on 9 March, 1786, the Duke of Clarence was given the Freedom of the town.

A number of historic expeditions left from Plymouth at this time. Captain Cook sailed from Plymouth on all his voyages. In 1768, he left in the *Endeavour* to sail round the world and in 1772, sailed for New Zealand in the *Resolution*. Captain Furneaux, of Swilly, was in the ship *Adventure* that went with Cook on that voyage. His voyage in the *Resolution*, which left in 1776 and during which, in 1779, he was killed, nearly did not start at all as the ships were almost wrecked under the Citadel. That, and many other shipwrecks, emphasised the need for a breakwater to provide shelter in the Sound. William Bligh, of the *Bounty*, was another famous person associated with the town. He was baptised in St Andrew's in October 1754, but was probably born in Cornwall. He became a successful naval captain and in 1787 was sent to the West Indies to introduce the bread-fruit plant. This was the voyage during which Fletcher Christian and a mutinous crew took over the ship and set Bligh and twenty castaways adrift in an open boat. It is remarkable that the castaways survived, as the boat drifted 4,000 miles to Timor.

During the many wars, spies and infiltrators were common in the towns. There were sabotage attempts in the Dockyard as French, Spanish and American agents tried to gain a little advantage. The most famous spy was Count de Parades, who by bribery managed to obtain the plans of the Dockyard and Citadel, which he passed to the French. This led to a projected assault on Plymouth by a combined French and Spanish fleet of sixty six ships and 30,000 men. They anchored in Cawsand Bay on 6 August 1779 and the town made hasty, if somewhat inadequate, precautions. Old cannon were dragged out and placed in prominent positions, a boom was erected across the Cattewater and prisoners of war were dispersed around the area. A storm on 21 August drove the ships into open water and in sight of Sir Charles Hardy, who was cruising in the channel with a small group of naval ships. The French fleet, although with superior numbers, backed away from a confrontation and sailed for France without firing a shot.

The end of the American War of Independence in 1783 provided a brief period of peace before the flurry of activity at the end of the century with the French Revolution and renewed hostilities with France. In May 1794, Lord Howe had left the Sound to attack and crush the French Fleet off Brest. A certain sailor named Nelson was making a name for himself in these sea battles and on 17 January 1801 was promoted to Vice-Admiral. He hoisted his flag first on the *San Joseph*, in the fleet under the Earl of St Vincent, anchored in the Sound. Nelson was honoured with the Freedom of the City of Exeter on 21 January and on the 22nd he received a letter from the Mayor of Plymouth offering him the Freedom of the Borough. The news of peace in 1801 was welcomed with wild jubilation. Bonfires were lit, firework displays held and 4,000 dockyardmen marched in procession, but the celebrations were short-lived as hostilities were renewed in May 1803. The news of the Battle of Trafalgar, in 1805, was received with pride at the victory, and sadness at the death of Nelson. Theatre performances were interrupted when the news was received from despatches, landed in Plymouth, on their way to London.

A number of unsavoury incidents occurred in Plymouth at the end of the century. Press gangs were busy, there was a shortage of food and prices were high. Mobs pillaged shops and attacked tradesmen and a full-scale riot was only allayed when Mayor Langmead persuaded the Government to allow army and naval supplies to be sold to the general public. Naval mutinies also occurred. They started at Spithead in 1797 but soon spread to the other naval ports. In Plymouth and the Dockyard, officers were turned off their ships and some were dropped in the harbour. Mobs rampaged through the towns and the mutiny was only quelled when Admiral Lord Keith addressed the men in person.

Other incidents marked this period, two of them concerning members of the Pellew family. Sir Edward Pellew, of the *Indefatigable*, was on his way to dine with a Dr Hawker, on 25 January 1796, when he saw a crowd of people rushing to the Hoe. An East India transport, the *Dutton*, had been thrown on the rocks below the Citadel by heavy seas. When Sir Edward Pellew reached the scene, there was utter chaos and no-one seemed able to offer any help. The crew of the *Dutton* appeared to have given up hope. Seizing a rope, Pellew was hauled through the water to the ship, took command and, by using hawsers and cradles, effected the rescue of nearly 600 passengers and crew. For this action he was given the Freedom of Plymouth and created a baronet. He later became an admiral and in 1814 was made Viscount Exmouth. The other incident involved his brother, Admiral Sir Israel Pellew, then captain of the frigate *Amphion*. On 24 September, 1796, while moored in the Hamoaze, the ship was torn apart by a terrific explosion. Sir Israel Pellew was knocked into the water unconscious but he and his lieutenant, who was blown through a window, were saved. Only 17 out of 220 men survived.

Thousands of prisoners had been captured during the French and American wars and the numbers that were brought to Plymouth far exceeded the capacity of the prison at Millbay. In 1762 there were 7,000 housed at Millbay and elsewhere. Millbay prison became overcrowded, insanitary, food was bad and there were numerous escapes. On one occasion 150 prisoners escaped by digging a tunnel. Hulks moored in the Hamoaze were used for the overspill; the *Royal Oak* in 1759, *San Rafael* in 1778 and the *El Firme* in 1809. But there were still too many prisoners to house, and Sir Thomas Tyrwhitt, MP for Plymouth, as part of his plan for the development of Dartmoor, had a prison built at Princetown. The first prisoners were transferred there in 1809 and by 1813 it held 1,700 American and 8,000 French prisoners. The prison cemeteries indicate that over 1,400 prisoners died while at Princetown. The prison was used again in 1855 during the Crimean War. The plight of the Americans was remembered by the 'Daughters of 1812' who undertook restoration of the doorway of the Prysten House as a memorial.

The war era was brought to a close by the exploits of Wellington and the capture of Napoleon. Wellington had embarked from Plymouth in 1812 on his way to his battle and victory at Salamanca. Napoleon was finally captured on board the *Bellerophon* at Rochefort and brought first to Torbay and then to Plymouth. The ship, and the occasional glimpse of Napoleon, provided great interest and excitement for the local population for a few weeks. As soon as Napoleon's fate was decided the *Bellerophon*, known somewhat affectionately by the locals as the *Billy Ruffin*, sailed from the Sound. *The Bellerophon* was renamed the *Captivity* and returned to use as a convict ship before being broken up in 1832. Some of the ship's timber was used by Dr George Bellamy, one-time surgeon on the *Bellerophon*, as part of a new cottage he built at Plymstock.

The sea and the exploits of Plymouth men and ships dominate Plymouth's past. Everyday life was also dominated by the sea and coastal shipping, as travel by road was difficult. It was much easier to sail from London than it was to travel overland. But the 18th century marked the beginning of major improvements to inland communications, consolidated in the following century. It was generally assumed that each parish had to maintain its own roads but this clearly hindered the development of important national routes. To improve this situation, the first Turnpike Act was passed in 1663, empowering private trusts to recover the costs of improving the roads by charging tolls. Roads were improved and toll houses, with gates or pikes, appeared at regular intervals. The gates were opened or pikes turned on payment of the tolls. Many roads emanating from London had been turnpiked by 1750, but the Great West Road to Plymouth was not one of them. There was much local support to remedy this situation and, in May 1753, the Act was passed allowing turnpikes as far west as Exeter. The improvements were left to trusts set up by towns on the route and the Exeter Act allowed for improvement of the road to Chudleigh Bridge. Chudleigh Bridge was linked west by the Ashburton Trust to South Brent and the Plymouth East Trust finally completed the chain to Gasking Gate, Plymouth. The new road was completed in 1758 and superseded the 'old' route to Exeter via Tavistock and Okehampton. The first regular service to Exeter was operated by John Bignell, the landlord of the Prince George Inn, in Vauxhall Street. Journey time was twelve hours.

Other roads were swiftly improved; the Modbury turnpike through Yealmpton to the main road at Plympton (1759), the Cremyll-Liskeard road (1760), thence by other Acts to Penzance, and roads from Tavistock to Callington, Launceston, Lydford and to Plymouth via Yelverton. Changes were also taking place to the roads in and between the towns of Plymouth, Stonehouse and Plymouth Dock. In 1767 an Act was passed which empowered Lord Mount Edgcumbe and Sir John St Aubyn to build a bridge over Stonehouse Creek. Because of the cost, they and their heirs were given the right to collect tolls. Pedestrians were charged ½d and the bridge became known as the halfpenny bridge. On the east side of Plymouth, Lord Boringdon had reclaimed some of the Plympton marshes to build a road to his house at Saltram, and he also promoted the Plymouth Embankment Company which drained the Laira marshes and permitted the new embankment road from Crabtree to Plymouth. The final link in the new route, between Breton Side and Embankment Road, was opened in the 1810 Jubilee year of George III.

Travel in and around Plymouth was developing apace with the new turnpikes. Carriages were in operation in 1775 and ran regular services from Old Town to Fore Street, Plymouth Dock for a fare of 1s. Sedan chairs were in use and cost 6d for short journeys. Other forms of transport, such as hackney coaches and chaises, were developing rapidly. In 1796, William Birch of Stoke Damerel introduced a coach service from Plymouth to Exeter. The town was also building up its commerce and industry. One of the chief industries was the manufacture of woollens, especially by the Shepherd family. They had factories close by the quay near Coxside and mills at Buckfastleigh, Ashburton, Tavistock and Totnes. William Shepherd, who ran the enterprises at the end of the 18th century, was something of a philanthropist and one-tenth of the profits were divided among the poor. He also provided his employees with loans. Another important industrialist was William Cookworthy, who invented and manufactured Plymouth china. It is said that he discovered suitable 'china clay' materials on his journeys in Cornwall. Until then, coarse brown and yellow earthenware and finer cream coloured ware was produced by the two firms of Alsop and Mellier, from premises at Coxside. Cookworthy received a patent for his chinaware in 1768 and it is believed that the first example dates from March of that year. The china was characteristically plain white but some pieces were decorated with coral and shells. The whereabouts of the manufactory is uncertain but Cookworthy resided in a Queen Anne house on the north side of Notte Street. The business moved to Bristol in 1774 and then the patent was transferred to a Staffordshire Company.

Some industries were declining and others growing. Sugar refining had ceased by 1800, but brewing was increasing. Salt had always been made locally and in 1814 the Lower Street salt refinery closed, but Ogg's salt works in Breton Side, near where the Salvation Army building now stands, was still prosperous and existed until 1857. It was a boom time for housebuilders, with the town expanding eastwards along the Exeter Road and northwards to Regent and Cobourg Streets. George Street was commenced in 1776 and consisted of a pleasant series of suburban residences. It was remarked of one professional gentleman, who had built a house at its far end, that he could never expect his clients to come so far to see him.

A number of Plymouth's famous schools were established in the 17th and 18th centuries to meet the needs of the growing towns. Schools founded in the 18th century were the Grey Coat School, the Household of Faith and Lady Rogers' School. Plympton Grammar School, a private foundation, was completed in 1671. This school was famous in the 18th century for a headmaster named Samuel Reynolds and for the attendance of his son, Joshua. Northcote was another famous artist of that school. A meeting held in Plymouth Guildhall in 1809 put forward a plan for the establishment of a Public School. This resulted in a boys' school being opened near the Pig Market in Bedford Street. It moved to Cobourg Street in 1812 and was joined by a girls' school, established under the same agreement. A committee, working on similar lines, established a school in St John Street, Plymouth Dock in about 1799. Stoke Public School dates from 1809 and schools in Stonehouse existed in Quarry Street and Union Lane.

Plymouth, Plymouth Dock and Stonehouse at the end of the Napoleonic era, were developing between them into a major provincial centre. Schools, theatres, hotels, industry and trade were all expanding and the scene was set for continued growth in the 19th century, the coming of the railway and the amalgamation of the three settlements.

LEFT: Main gate at Plymouth Citadel. RIGHT: Decorated side entrance to the Citadel.

ABOVE: Plymouth and the Citadel in 1710. (LS) BELOW: Jacobean Guildhall. (LS)

View of the Mayoralty House. From the new Quay

On Friday, *February* the 10th, 1758,
Will be perform'd
A Concert of MUSICK,
Divided into several Parts.
BOXES 3s. PIT 2s. GALLERY 1s.

TICKETS to be had at Bingham's Coffee-House, the *Red Lion* in *Southside-street*, the *Pope's-Head* in *Pike-street*, the *Prince George* on *Foxhole-Key*, and at the *Flow Tavern* on the *New Key*.

The Curtain to be drawn up precisely at Six o'Clock.

Between the Parts of the CONCERT will be perform'd gratis

The ROMAN FATHER:

As it is now revived at the Theatre-Royal in *Drury-Lane*, with universal Applause.

Written by W. WHITEHEAD, Esq; præter Poet-Laureat.

Roman Father		Mr. Cooke,
Turfus Hoftilius		Mr. Jenkins,
Publius	by	Mr. Gates,
Valerius		Mr. Fitzmaurice,
Soldier		Mr. Holland.

CITIZENS, by Mr. *Fowles*, Mr. *Cartwright*, and others

Horatia	by	Mrs. Price,
Valeria		Mrs. Maxson.

With the Triumphant Entry of Publius, properly attended with the Roman Insignia, and all other Decorations entirely new.

To which will be added a BALLAD FARCE, call'd

THE LOTTERY.

Jack Stocks, alias Lord Lace, by Mr. *Pitt*, old Stocks Mr. *Cartwright*, Lovemore Mr. *White*, Chloe, alias Lady Lace Mrs. *Maxson*.

. No Persons to be admitted behind the Scenes.

PLYMOUTH: Printed by ANDREW BRICE, on the New-Key.

To the Public.

ON maturely confidering the Nature of the RESOLUTIONS figned by us the 6th Inftant, which were haftily adopted, under the Impreffion of popular Threats, and without well weighing the Confequence to the Public. we think it neceffary now to ftate. that they have already had the evil Effect of caufing the Supplies of FLOUR and CORN intended for this Port, from the Coaft of *Hampfhire* and *Suffex*, to be ordered to other Markets ; and we have too much Reafon to fear, that if our Refolution not to give more than Three Guineas per Sack be adhered to, it will effectually prevent other Supplies from reaching this Place :

WE THEREFORE RESOLVE,

FIRST—Contrary to our anxious Defire, we find it utterly impoffible to obtain any FLOUR at the Prices mentioned in our former Publication, and we fhall be under the Neceffity of fhutting our Shops if perfifted in.

SECONDLY—That although we are anxious to purchafe Flour upon the *loweft Terms* ; yet, we are convinced, that unlefs we give a Price equal to other Markets, we fhall not receive the ufual Supply neceffary for the Accommodation of the Public.

LASTLY—Relying with Confidence on the Magiftrates for Protection, while in the legal Exercife of our Bufinefs, we fhall continue our Trade as ufual ; and at all Times fhew a Readinefs to come forward with the reft of our Townfmen for the Relief of the Diftreffed.

SIGNED,

Thomas Mumford,	William Hare,	James Dinnis,
George Bond,	B. Cofway,	William Sherril,
William Williams,	John Kingdom,	Benjamin Pearn,
N. Crimp, junior,	G. Stooke,	William Dyer,
John Kelir,	W. Yeoland,	John Wage,
John Butcher,	Benjamin Denfcam,	William Caffentine,
William Arthur,	William Morgan,	John Cooling,
Matthew Lapp,	John Smale,	John Cayzer,
Richard Frean,	James Ryan,	George Elms,
John Weftlake,	John Grebbell,	Robert Hufband,
William Spry,	George Full,	James Mitchell,
Thomas Tanner,	William Chenoweth,	Henry May,
Nicholas Carter,	John Bray,	John Sarell.

Dated April 10, 1801.

NETTLETON, PRINTER, PLYMOUTH.

ABOVE: Old Mayoralty House, Woolster Street. (LS)BELOW: Theatre bill showing tickets for Drury Lane, sold in local inns. (LS) RIGHT: Early attempt to resist price rises in flour. (MS)

ABOVE: Local trade coinage of the 18th century. (MS) BELOW: Plymouth
bank note, dated 25 March 1824. (MS)

ABOVE: Congestion in Plymouth Dock, 1785. (LS) LEFT: Diving bell used
in the construction of a sea-wall. (LS) RIGHT: View of Devonport Dockyard
from Mount Edgcumbe. (LS)

The Rise of Devonport

Plymouth had always been an important place for the assembly and provisioning of the National Fleet, but did not possess a Navy Yard. Shipbuilding and repairing had been undertaken by a number of private concerns operating on the shores of the Cattewater and at Saltash, such as the small ship repair base and ropewalk that existed at Teats Hill, Cattedown. Refitting was also carried out from a hulk established in the Cattewater by Cromwell. In 1663 the Navy Board orderd the sale of the hulk and the construction of shipyards, but the yards were never built and the hulk was repaired and continued to be used to refit ships. As early as Elizabethan times, Raleigh had proposed the Hamoaze as a naval harbour and some later schemes looked at Saltash as a likely base. These schemes came to nothing, largely because of objections from fishermen and from local inhabitants, who argued a naval yard would spoil their gardens and views.

Royal shipyards were concentrated at this time on the Thames and Medway estuaries and at Portsmouth. The need for another Royal Yard, further west, was emphasised after the Dutch raided the Medway in 1667, but no positive action was taken until, paradoxically, William came to the throne. After some initial debate, when alternative sites at Milford Haven, Falmouth and many Devon ports were considered, the Cattewater was chosen; later to be changed to the eastern side of the Hamoaze. Plans were drawn up in 1689 and the dock began in 1691 at Froward Point. The site was two miles from Plymouth, partly on the Mount Wise estate, and was separated from the town by marshes near the present Union Street. Thus, at the onset, the naval yards were not associated with Plymouth and access, for a number of years, was easiest by sea. The first docks were completed in 1693 and other buildings followed rapidly. A row of thirteen officers' houses was built on a terrace overlooking the docks, a large storehouse appeared on the point and a roofed ropehouse, 1,056 feet long, was added in 1698.

Plymouth at first ignored the new docks but, by 1698, when the cost of the works had risen to £70,000, it was forced to take notice. The number of workers employed in the docks steadily rose and it was clear that a new town was in its infancy and was likely to provide strong competition for Plymouth. At first new housing failed to keep pace with the number of workers and men were forced to lodge on ships anchored in the Hamoaze. One of the hindrances to the establishment of further housing was the refusal, until 1700, of the Morice trustees to part with any land for housing. The owner of the land, Sir Nicholas Morice, was a boy of thirteen when the first dock was built and his trustees would not sell. Eventually land was released and the first house built at North Corner and by 1733 Plymouth Dock had 3,000 inhabitants and was growing on a gridiron pattern of streets, with Fore Street as the main axis.

The great activity in the town was described vividly by Daniel Defoe in his *Tour Through England and Wales*. Trades-people and workmen flocked to the place and it grew so rapidly that Defoe suggested this was at the expense of Plymouth. Plymouth Dock had grown from nothing to half the population of Plymouth in fifty years. Its past is reflected in the parish church of Stoke Damerel; it was enlarged several times in the 18th century to meet the needs of the growing parish. A second aisle was built early in the century and, in 1730, the north aisle was added with generous help from Richard Young, a Dockyard officer. Extensive reconstruction was carried out in 1750 and financial assistance sought from the Admiralty. No money was forthcoming but materials were offered; thus, ships' masts were used as pillars, ships' beams as roof trusses and cabin fitments as doors. The memorials in the church reflect the type of parish, with Army and Naval officers, seamen, gunners and others concerned with the military prominent. In the 18th century Stoke Damerel Church, on a hill, overlooked Deadlake (Stonehouse Creek) on the shores of which for a number of years there stood a gibbet. It was the custom to allow the bodies to swing for a long time, over seven years in the case of William Smith and John Richards, who murdered a clerk in the Dockyard. The churchyard was also the focus of attention for body snatchers, stealing bodies for sale for anatomical studies. By 1801 Plymouth Duck had overtaken Plymouth in size and in 1821 their respective populations were some 35,000 and 21,000.

Relations between Plymouth and the Dock were strained and they argued continuously over many things, water supply being one. The growing town of Plymouth Dock was desperately in need of a clean water supply and in 1766, Sir John St Aubyn, lord of the manor of Stoke Damerel, offered to pay Plymouth Corporation £200 a year for the supply of water, but this was refused. The problem was solved in 1796 when the Dockers formed their own water company and ran another leat, near Drake's leat, from Dartmoor. It was always a working class town and wages were generally low, although the workers were allowed a number of perks such as wood chippings. Wages were brought by frigate from London once a quarter to avoid highwaymen — a period of rapid spending and celebration. However, the intervening periods were difficult and people soon ran up large debts. Social provisions were poor, largely because of the speed with which the town grew. At first there were no schools, no charities and medical provision was scanty. The market was in a wooden construction outside the yard gates and apparently many people preferred the market at Saltash, although it involved crossing the Tamar by ferry. There was little interaction with Plymouth. Churches were gradually built by public subscription; St Aubyn in 1771-2 and St John in 1797. Methodism grew, especially with the frequent visits of the Wesleys, and was always stronger in Dock than in Plymouth. Methodist churches were established at Ker Street in 1786 and in Morice Square in 1811, but nonconformists were often frowned upon by naval authorities and a Unitarian chapel in George Street, Dock, was closed in 1806 by the dockyard authorities. It is now the Old Chapel Public house. Roman Catholic chapels appeared in 1801 and 1807.

Wars with Spain, France, the American Colonies and the emerging United States created conditions for the sustained growth of the Dock. The dockyard extended across new land to the south, the original ropehouse was demolished and a new one built with a mast pond, new store, boat houses and two new slips. A third dry dock, the North Dock, was added in 1762. Other developments were taking place. Land on the shores of Stonehouse Creek was bought from Lord Edgcumbe and a new naval hospital built, designed in small blocks, enabling groups of patients to be isolated. It was completed in 1762. The architect was Alexander Rowehead and the hospital was the earliest example in the country with a limited number of patients in each block. It comprised eleven large and four smaller buildings, forming a square but separated to allow the free circulation of air. The hospital could be reached direct by boats from Stonehouse Creek, but this jetty closed after World War I and access is now only possible from the front gates. Two French scientists, Jaques Tenon and Charles-Augustin Coulomb visited a great many hospitals in Europe, including the Naval Hospital on 11-14 July, 1787, preferring it above all others. Thus it became the model for many French hospitals. It possesses many interesting features in its grounds such as a pay office, a chapel, a sundial made by John Gilbert of London, an octagonal water tower constructed of rubble and an octagonal, private post-box.

Other major building projects followed. In 1782, new blocks for the Royal Marines were built in Stonehouse; the more familiar blocks in Durnford Street were not added until 1857. Work on the fourth dry dock, planned to be the biggest in the country, was begun in 1789 and George III took great interest in it and came to see it under construction. One of the first ships to use it was the French *Commerce de Marseille*, captured in 1793, just after the outbreak of war with France.

The Hamoaze was a magnificent harbour, 5-6 miles long and up to a mile wide with numerous creeks and inlets and the deep channel, although narrow near Devils Point, was perfectly adequate. But there were two drawbacks. The Sound and entrance to the Hamoaze were unprotected, apart from a little shelter provided by Drake's Island, and the jagged Eddystone reefs were a perpetual danger to shipping. A breakwater was proposed in 1788 but it was not until 1806 that Lord St Vincent, the First Sea Lord, ordered detailed plans from John Rennie, a civil engineer. These were accepted and the first stone laid on the sea-floor on 12 August 1817. It was 25 years before the breakwater was finally complete, during which time a number of changes had to be made to the original plans. The Government bought 27 acres of limestone cliff at Oreston from the Duke of Bedford, and trains of trucks took the rock to specially constructed wharves, where they were run onto vessels fitted with rails and tipping devices. The original plan was to create the breakwater with a slope of 1 in 3 but a storm in 1817 shifted the rock and altered the slope to 1 in 5. The same thing happened in another storm in 1824 and the plans were altered to accommodate a slope of 1 in 5. That last storm, in which 25 ships were driven ashore, reinforced the need. The decreased slope meant that an extra 200,000 tons of stone were required, adding considerably to the time and cost. The breakwater, when finished, had taken 4 million tons of limestone and 3 million tons of granite facing blocks at a cost of £1.5 million. It included a central straight section, 3,000 feet long and, with its angled wings, its total length was over a mile.

The building of the lighthouses on the Eddystone reef is a saga in its own right. In the middle 17th century, two Plymouth citizens, Sir John Coryton and Mr H. Bunker petitioned Trinity House to erect a lighthouse, but were refused. In the ensuing years ships, both naval and private, continued to be wrecked with considerable loss of life and cargo. Public opinion was hardening and, with representations from London merchants, pressure was put on Trinity House until a Patent Roll was signed by William and Mary on 22 June 1694. The practical problems involved in the construction of a lighthouse were enormous and there appeared to be only one rock that possessed a possible building surface and was high enough to remain exposed at high water. Henry Winstanley of Littlebury, Essex, was chosen as designer and builder. The first summer was spent in creating 12 holes in which to fix iron stanchions. The project almost foundered then and there. The workmen, after rowing for anything up to 8 hours to reach the reef, found the rock too hard for their hand picks and were often so wet with flying spray that they could not even grip them. But the holes were finished on time and the iron stanchions fixed. The following summer was spent in creating a round pillar, 12 feet high and 14 feet in diameter, for the base of the lighthouse. The transference of stones by block and tackle from bobbing boats was extremely difficult and dangerous. Additional hazards were provided by marauding French ships and, on one occasion, despite naval protection, Winstanley was captured and taken to France. He was released after a fortnight and the work recommenced. The lighthouse, a polygonal tower with an open gallery near the top, was completed in 1698. The night of Friday 26 November 1703 is remembered all over England for the severity of the storm that occurred. Winstanley and some workmen had sailed to the lighthouse that night to effect some repairs caused by high seas the previous week. Just before midnight a terrific storm developed, causing incredible damage at sea and on land. The winds blew down houses, trees and chimneys over a wide area. The hundred feet spire of Stowmarket Church was blown over and the Bishop of Bath and Wells and his wife were killed by a falling chimney stack. Bristol lost goods worth £150,000 as a result of flooding caused by a wind tidal surge up the Severn Estuary. It has been estimated that over 800 houses were destroyed, 400 windmills blown down, seven church spires demolished and 123 people killed, while at sea, 150 ships were lost together with 8,000 sailors. At daybreak on Saturday there was no sign of the lighthouse and people at sea recalled seeing it engulfed by gigantic waves.

The next lighthouse, a round smooth tower of wood, was designed by Rudyerd. It was lit in 1708 and stood for 44 years until destroyed by fire on 2 December 1755. The three keepers, who made a valiant attempt to quench the fire, were rescued, but one of them, 94-year-old Henry Hall, looked up at the fire and was drenched by molten lead. When he died 14 days later a post-mortem revealed a 7 oz lead ingot in his stomach; he had clearly swallowed it.

John Smeaton built the next tower, with a core of Portland Stone and an outer casing of granite. It was curved like a tree trunk, lasted from 1759 to 1882 and was only dismantled because the sea was undermining the rock at its base. An alternative tower was built on an adjoining rock by Sir James Douglass and, when complete, Smeaton's tower was taken down and re-erected on the Hoe. The combination of lighthouse and breakwater made the harbours of Plymouth and Plymouth Dock among the safest in the country.

The growing population of Plymouth Dock needed careful nurturing but the settlement never came under a municipal administration. In 1780 the running of the town was shared by a Corps of Commissioners and the local Devon magistrates. It was growing rapidly and achieving a strong civic pride reflected in the spate of buildings designed by John Foulston. The first of his Devonport buildings was the Town Hall at the top of Ker Street, completed in 1821. It was financed as a private undertaking by a group of shareholders and consists of a large hall, which served as a magistrates' court and assembly room. Beneath the hall there were cells for prisoners, rooms for the police and the council chamber of the local Mechanics Institution. Another distinctive Foulston building in this group is the Egyptian building of 1823. It was originally intended as the Plymouth Dock and Stonehouse Classical and Mathematical School, but became the Civil and Military Library in 1827. It is an extremely unusual building with a rare architectural style. Foulston added the Mount Zion Chapel which, in his own words was 'a variety of oriental architecture'.

In the same year, 1823, Plymouth Dock petitioned George IV for permission to change the name of the town. This was granted and on 1 January 1824, the name Devonport was used officially for the first time. As a lasting memorial, Foulston's 124 feet high Doric column was built. It appears that the column is aligned with Union Street, linking Stonehouse with Plymouth perhaps as a provocative gesture to the inhabitants of the latter. This was certainly in the mind of an anonymous poet, reported by Trewin (1973):

> 'Plymouth's in a mighty bother,
> To find her whelp desert her mother
> Then some grand scheme they 'gan to ponder
> To strike the gaping mob with wonder,
> The fine great project seemed to swell 'em
> When all their brains hatched out a column'.

Monumental architecture was also included in the plans for the Royal William Victualling Yard, Stonehouse, designed by Sir John Rennie. It occupies 14 acres, six of which were recovered from the sea of Stonehouse Creek. The main facade is the north front of three parallel buildings, the centre one with a cupola. The gateway from the south end of Cremyll Street is impressive and is surmounted by a 13 feet figure of William IV.

Stonehouse and Devonport were joined together as a Parliamentary Borough electing two Members of Parliament, in 1832. The first members were Sir George Grey and Sir Edward Codrington. There was little enthusiasm for a separate town at first but Plymouth continually turned away from thoughts of amalgamation. Devonport elected its first full Town Council in the year of Queen Victoria's accession and its first mayor was Edward St Aubyn, Lord of the Manor of Stoke Damerel. Stonehouse, at this time, was running out of space. Its 20,000 inhabitants were squeezed between Plymouth, Stonehouse Creek, the Victualling Yard and the Royal Naval Hospital. It eventually acquired a Local Board which developed into an Urban Council under the Act of 1894. All three settlements were virtually contiguous and the story of the 19th century is one of increasing pressure on space and the ultimate necessity to formalise amalgamation.

LEFT: Smeaton's Tower, completed in 1759, from an engraving of 1763. (LS) RIGHT: Fire in the Dockyard, 27 September 1840. (LS) BELOW: St Michael's Terrace, Stoke in the early 19th century. (LS)

LEFT: Royal William Victualling Yard, Stonehouse. RIGHT: John Foulston's Devonport column. BELOW: Trade card of William Hook, draper, Market Street, Devonport. (LS)

46

ABOVE: Devonport Town Hall, Column and Egyptian building, all designed by John Foulston. BELOW: Corn measures, Stoke Damerel parish. (MS)

ABOVE: Plymouth and Drake's Island from Mount Edgecumbe. BELOW:
The Hoe and Citadel, with the start of a regatta. (LS)

Three Towns Into One

The 19th century was a period of intense activity in the three towns of Plymouth, Stonehouse and Devonport. Population increased rapidly, placing tremendous pressures on the housing stock, water supply, transport services, medical and educational facilities, pressures which the authorities found difficult to meet. It was a time of social contrast, with the rich embarking on grand building schemes and the poor cramped together in overcrowded, insanitary housing. Technological innovation in industry and transport, especially steam power on land and at sea, was opening up new prospects. These numerous threads produce a complicated tapestry of events and some need to be disentangled to produce a coherent story. The growth of the commercial docks and the build-up of the international liner trade were intimately connected with the arrival of the railways; a separate strand. The physical growth and changing appearance of Plymouth, Stonehouse and Devonport and the pressures that led to their amalgamation in 1914, are another.

Growth of the three towns was phenomenal. In 1801 the total population of Plymouth was 19,040 and that of Devonport 23,747 but, by the outbreak of the First World War, the combined population, including Stonehouse, was approximately 209,000. Between 1841 and 1851 the population of Plymouth had increased by over 1,600 a year, in large measure due to migration from West Devon and Cornwall, prompted by low agricultural wages and the closure of Cornish mines. This rate of increase was not matched, however, by the building of new houses, and serious overcrowding resulted. The average occupancy rate in the 1850s was ten people to a house, much higher than London or other major cities. In some parts of the town the rate was even higher, with houses at the top of New Street accommodating an average of twenty four people. Contemporary accounts present a grim picture. H. Woolcombe, writing in 1812, noted that the style of buildings was bad and appeared to be getting worse. A medical report by Dr Rawlinson, in 1853, was even more disturbing, noting that many of the old back streets were narrow and steep, with dirty surface-drainage channels down their centres. Many houses, formerly occupied by gentry, were in a state of disrepair and used by vagrants and vandals. Rooms in many houses were subdivided and one privy often served a whole block. Water supply was totally inadequate with one standpipe, operating for only one hour a day, supplying an entire court. In some streets there were no drains at all and Claremont Street, off King Street, possessed one privy to every sixty-six occupants. The worst slums were in Stonehouse, around Long Street, and in the New Street and Breton Side area of Plymouth.

It is hardly surprising that outbreaks of smallpox, cholera, diptheria and scarlet fever were frequent. One smallpox outbreak in 1872 killed 448 people. The big killer was cholera and outbreaks in 1832 and 1849 claimed 1,031 and 1,894 victims respectively. These were major epidemics but cholera claimed high death rates in many other years. Religious and political leaders pressed for improvements. George Soltau, the Liberal leader, was involved in the formation of the Plymouth Branch of the Health of Towns Association, and the Unitarian minister, Rev W.J. Odgers, had for a number of years reported the serious state of the town's slums. It was Rev Odgers who was instrumental in getting the public bath houses opened in Hoegate Street in 1850. The medical situation was improved by some local doctors, who, through their Medical Society, opened an eye hospital in 1821 at Millbay and the South Devon and East Cornwall Hospital in Notte Street in 1840. The authorities were slow to respond but eventually, in 1854, Plymouth adopted the 1848 Public Health Act. Devonport did not respond until 1866. Better drains were installed, streets widened and houses pulled down. The major problem was still a lack of suitable housing because slum clearance merely put greater pressure on the better housing. The problem was not alleviated until the Housing of the Working Class Act of 1890 compelled local authorities to act. Plymouth Council then set up a committee for housing and the first Council houses were built in 1896 in Laira Bridge Road. In Devonport, a private Dockyard Dwelling Company was formed which began a series of slum clearance schemes.

The housing pressure resulted in gaps between and within the towns being infilled, together with an outward spread into the surrounding countryside. In Devonport, a working class suburb developed at Morice Town and the villages of Lower and Higher Stoke grew and coalesced. A syndicate of builders developed the Keyham Barton area, north of St Leven Road, and sold houses for £200. More substantial villas spread from Higher Stoke and Molesworth Road and joined developments from Millbridge and Pennycomequick. Growth also took place towards Weston Mill and Devonport expanded further by taking in St Budeaux in 1898, and Pennycross in 1899.

The site of Stonehouse had always been a cramped one with limited space for development. The Durnford area was infilled with small working class houses and the old Sourpool marshes were drained. Houses then extended eastwards towards Plymouth. The elegant Wyndham Square was built to designs by Foulston in anticipation, falsely as it turned out, that Eldad might become the heart of the three towns.

The growth of Plymouth was constrained by a number of large private estates. The Barley House Estate, from King Street to North Road, did not become available for development until the late 1860s and on the east, adjoining Beaumont Park, the Culme-Seymour family estate was not developed until the end of the 19th century. This meant that housing was forced to spread north to North Road and Cobourg Street, up to North Hill, down Alexandra Road and along Mutley Plain. More substantial residences were built from Mannamead down Townsend hill to Hyde Park Corner. The town also took in surrounding villages and in 1896 the boundaries were extended officially to include Compton. Eventually, by the early 20th century, the town was filled from Tothill to Lipson, Prince Rock to Cattedown, Mutley to Mannamead and to Peverell Park Road, while new developments reached into Beacon Park.

The town centres were changing as much as their suburbs. Like Devonport, the centre of Plymouth was also to be influenced by Foulston. In January 1810, a competition, organised by Edmund Lockyer, was announced for designs for a tavern, ballroom and theatre in three distinct buildings. The competition was won by Foulston, who had submitted a design bringing all three elements together. The main 268 feet frontage facing Georges Place was dominated by a portico with 30 feet high Ionic columns. The theatre lay to the west of the portico and the ballroom and hotel to the east. The hotel contained suites of rooms for between twenty and thirty families, a large dining room, coffee room, commercial room, billiard room and thirteen smaller dining rooms. The Theatre Royal was separated from the hotel by thick walls to prevent a fire hazard. The auditorium was similarly separated from the general circulation areas. The entire inner structure was of cast iron and it was, according to Foulston, the only fire-proof theatre in the country. The auditorium was capable of accommodating 1,192 people in a three-quarter circle. Foulston's second public building in Plymouth was the Proprietary Library in Cornwall Street, after which he prepared a design for an Exchange which was never adopted, although an exchange was eventually built in Woolster Street. His next major commission was the Athenaeum (1818-19) for the Plymouth Institution. This was built in temple-like form to the west of the Theatre Royal. In the next five years Foulston was designing and building in Devonport but returned to Plymouth in 1823 to design St Catherine's Chapel, facing the eastern wing of the Royal Hotel. In 1826 he was commissioned to restore St Andrew's Church but this work was obliterated by the later restoration of Sir Gilbert Scott.

Other building schemes continued throughout the Victorian era. The building of a new Guildhall, beside St Andrew's Church, was completed in 1873 and the old Guildhall in Whymple Street became a free library. A number of churches date from this time: Holy Trinity (1840), Christ Church (1845), St James (1861) and King Street Methodist Church (1864). Baptist churches were built at George Street (1845) and Mutley (1864) and a Congregationalist church at Sherwell (1864). The increasing population meant that new schools were desperately needed, especially at infant and junior levels. Charles Church started two schools; one in 1836, which moved to Tavistock Place in 1846, and a second in 1856 in the Mount Street area. Other church schools followed: St Andrew's in 1842, Holy Trinity in 1844 and St Peter and Christ Church in 1850.

There were social and intellectual activities in the towns to suit all tastes. Plymouth Races took place every August on Chelson Meadow, and in November the Plymouth fair was held around the market. Yacht clubs and regattas were becoming important elements in town life. The Royal Western Yacht Club was formed in 1827 and in 1866 moved to its present premises at West Hoe. A number of educational and academic institutions were also established. The Plymouth Institution met at the Athenaeum and the Plymouth Proprietary Library existed in Cornwall Street. Mechanics Institutes and YMCAs opened in both Devonport and Plymouth. The Marine Biological Association and Aquarium opened in 1885 on the Hoe and soon built up a world-wide reputation for scientific research. Plymouth started a museum in Beaumont House but moved it to the present site in Tavistock Road in 1910. A slightly different but equally beneficial facility appeared in Devonport when Agnes 'Aggie' Weston opened the first of her Sailor's Rests, in 1876 outside the Dockyard gates in Fore Street.

These developments enabled writers in the 1890s to remark on the considerable improvements that had taken place and to express the opinion that Plymouth was, as well managed as any provincial town. Money was being spent, not only on new housing, but on public parks, recreation grounds, and accommodation for bathers. The Hoe had been almost doubled in extent and laid out with gardens and paths. Plymothians could boast one of the most magnificent promenades in the Kingdom, especially when the Hoe became the site for many memorials. The Boehm statue of Drake was erected in 1884 and the foundation stone for the Armada memorial was laid in 1888, the year of the tercentenary celebrations. But despite these considerable improvements, water supply was still a problem and the increasing urban sprawl required an efficient transport system.

Plymouth had built a number of reservoirs: Sherwell in the 1820s, (3.6m gallons), Crownhill in 1851 (1.1m gallons), Hartley 1859-62 (7.1m gallons) and Roborough in 1885 (1m gallons). But daily consumption in 1893 was estimated at about 4.5m gallons and Plymouth clearly needed more water. This was felt acutely when the open leat from Dartmoor froze, as it did in 1881. After much deliberation Burrator was chosen as the site for a new reservoir; it was operational by 1898. Stonehouse had always found water supply difficult and in the early days had relied on a leat from a stream at Torr. Later, storage reservoirs were built at Peverell and, until a few years ago, these could be seen in Central Park to the west of Peverell Park Road. Stonehouse was joined to the Plymouth supply in 1893. Devonport obtained water from Burrator Reservoir when the towns amalgamated in 1914 but, until then it had relied on its own leat bringing water from the West Dart, feeding storage reservoirs at Stoke and Crownhill.

The spread of suburbs, combined with the local topography, posed a number of problems for the transport systems. The route east to Plymstock was improved considerably by the construction of an iron bridge over the Laira Estuary. Designed by James Rendel, it was opened in 1827 and was, at the time, the second longest iron bridge in the country. Many creeks and inlets could not be bridged and Plymothians have had to rely heavily on ferry services of one form or another. Some of these have disappeared, such as the service from Phoenix Wharf to Hooe, Oreston and Turnchapel, but others, such as the Cremyll ferry, are a reminder of how important these services once were. The crossing to Cremyll dates back to at least the 12th century and John Wesley crossed on it in 1748 and 1768. The landing point on the Plymouth side was at Cremyll Point but, when this site was bought by the Admiralty for the new victualling yard, a new paved slipway was provided north of Admiral's Hard. The quay at Cremyll was built up in 1836-37 under the direction of James Rendel. Steam ferries appeared late on this route and an application to operate one was turned down in 1881 on the grounds that it could not produce a profit. But in 1884 a steam launch, the *Dodo*, was built for foot passengers and the service started in January 1885. A horseboat was also operated, usually towed by one of the passenger boats, having to be cast loose and poled ashore at Admiral's Hard.

An ancient ferry had also existed at Saltash, belonging to the manor of Trematon. This became inadequate and a chain suspension bridge was promoted in an advertisement dated 18 July 1823. This did not succeed, for lack of money, but in 1831 the Saltash Floating Bridge Company called in Rendel to introduce a similar floating bridge to the one he had installed on the River Dart. The ferry dragged itself across the river guided by heavy chains. A floating bridge system was introduced at Torpoint in 1834, causing so much competition that the Saltash Company went bankrupt. The Saltash service was resurrected in 1891, with a new steel ferry, and lasted until made obsolete by the Tamar Road Bridge.

R. C. Sambourne in *A hundred years of street travel*, points out that Plymouth had always been progressive in the field of road transport and horse drawn 'buses had been running as early as 1832. One of the first horse tramways in the British Isles was started on 18 March 1872 and linked Plymouth with Devonport. This first route was from Derry's Clock, through Stonehouse to Cumberland Gardens, Devonport, with passing places at Devonport Hill, Stonehouse Bridge and in Union Street. It was run on a 4ft 8½in gauge single track line by the Plymouth, Stonehouse and Devonport Tramways Company. The line was extended to the centre of Devonport, in 1874, by a one-way system, inwards up Chapel Street and outwards via St Aubyn Street. The terminus was in Fore Street at the junction of Marlborough Street and the initial fleet consisted of eight green and white liveried trams, each drawn by two horses. In 1880 the Plymouth, Devonport and District Tramways Company was set up, initially operating steam locomotives. This company ran a single line from Millbay Station via George Street, Lockyer Street, Princess Square, Bedford Street, Coborg Street and Houndiscombe Road, terminating at Hyde Park Corner. It used five locomotives hauling open-top cars but there were numerous complaints of noise, smoke, smells and bad timekeeping and the company was forced to sell out after one year. It was taken over by the Plymouth Tramways Company, who operated horse trams. In 1892 this company was bought for £12,500 and became the Plymouth Corporation Tramway Department, changing its livery to the famous vermilion, with white window pillars. Extensions were made in 1893 from Millbay Station to the Hoe and Piers, and from Mutley Plain to Compton Lane End. Trace horses for the steep climb up Townsend Hill were stabled at Belgrave Mews, later the site of the Belgrave Cinema.

Numerous horse 'bus services also existed, operated by private individuals. Baskervilles ran services to Roborough and to Salisbury Road and Mannamead. Andrews and Smith competed for custom between Derry's Clock and Fore Street, Devonport and Newcombe carried passengers between Millbay Station and Queens Gate, Lipson. Mills operated a service between St Andrew's Church and Stoke and from Millbay Station to Cattedown.

Local train services were started by the LSWR from St Budeaux to the Dockyard in 1890 and from Plymouth to Turnchapel and Yealmpton in 1897. The GWR responded by opening a series of halts between Saltash and Plympton in 1904. Ferries often linked with the railway network, one such link being the interesting service operated by the steamer *Kitley Belle* from the Steer Point Halt down the Yealm estuary to Newton Ferrers and Noss Mayo.

The arrival of electrification, at the turn of the century, revolutionised street transport. Plymouth Corporation received Royal assent to introduce electric traction in 1896 and the first route electrified, on 22 September 1899, was from the Theatre Royal to Prince Rock. Power was obtained from the new power station at Cattedown and electric street lighting was also provided, using similar standards to those of the tramway. The outer districts of Plymouth were developing rapidly and a double track extension was built in 1905 to Peverell Park Road, the new road to the Pounds Estate. The Devonport and District Tramway Company became a subsidiary of the British Electric Traction Group and started an electric network in 1901, running from Devonport to the developing areas of Millbridge, Stoke, Keyham and Camels Head. Power was obtained from the Devonport Corporation power station in Newport Street, Stonehouse, via a sub-station constructed to blend with the architecture of Devonport Technical School.

There were several early attempts to operate motor 'buses. The Plymouth Motor Company started a service in 1900 between Derry's Clock and Salisbury Road with five Daimlers and succeeded in driving Baskervilles off the route. In October 1909, Peverell Road Car Company ran 'buses on the Milehouse and Stoke route, garaging them in an old building known as Outland Mills at the junction of Lyndhurst and Milehouse Roads. This service was not a success and ceased in June 1911 and, until the end of the First World War, street travel was dominated by the electric tram. Free movement was considerably hampered by the toll gates. The gates at Milehouse, Mutley Plain and Cattedown Corner were closed in the 1850s but it was not until 1 April 1924 that the last toll points at Stonehouse Bridge, Millbridge, the Embankment and the Iron Bridge were ceremoniously closed by the Mayor, Solomon Stephens.

The physical growth of the three towns, with the jostling for areas in which to expand, led to many calls for an official amalgamation. One body which spoke out for amalgamation was the Plymouth Social Democratic Federation, which formed the Three Towns Housing Association. There had been strong calls for amalgamation in 1888 and a conference took place in Stonehouse Town Hall in 1902. A series of ballots in 1913 finally encouraged Plymouth to make formal representation for amalgamation. Plymouth Guildhall was the venue for an inquiry, opened on 28 January 1914. Plymouth's case was put by Town Clerk J. H. Ellis, and Major-General A. P. Penton, Officer-in-Command South West Coast Defences. One of the main arguments was that, in time of war, it would be advantageous to have only one authority. The German threat was looming, and, although Devonport objected, the arguments for amalgamation won and the three towns were united.

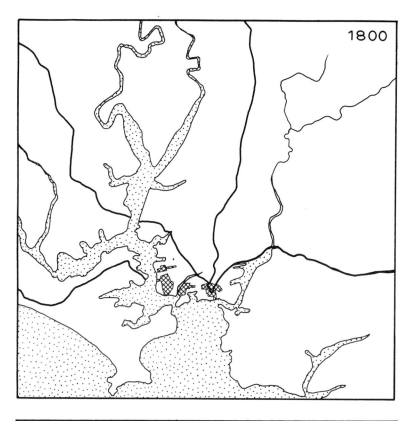

1800

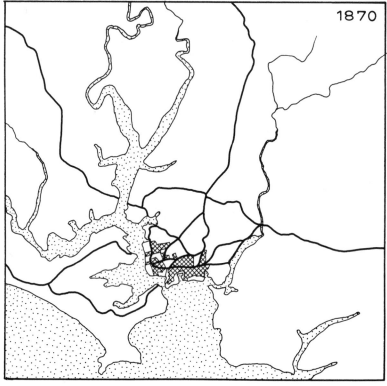

1870

54

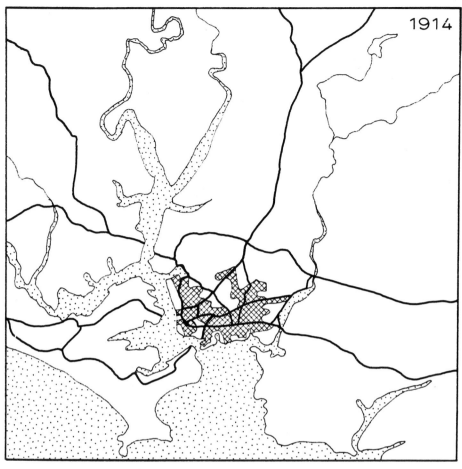

OPPOSITE ABOVE: The three towns still separate. BELOW: Room for expansion is limited. ABOVE: The three towns are one. BELOW: Derry's Clock and Royal Hotel, 19th century. (LS) LEFT: Derry's Clock.

LEFT: Devonport Town Hall. (LS) RIGHT: Stonehouse Town Hall before amalgamation. (LS) BELOW: Plymouth Barbican and Pool. (LS)

ABOVE: The Citadel in the late 19th century. (LS) LEFT: Plymouth
Guildhall, 1874. (LS) RIGHT: Notte Street, c1880. (LS)

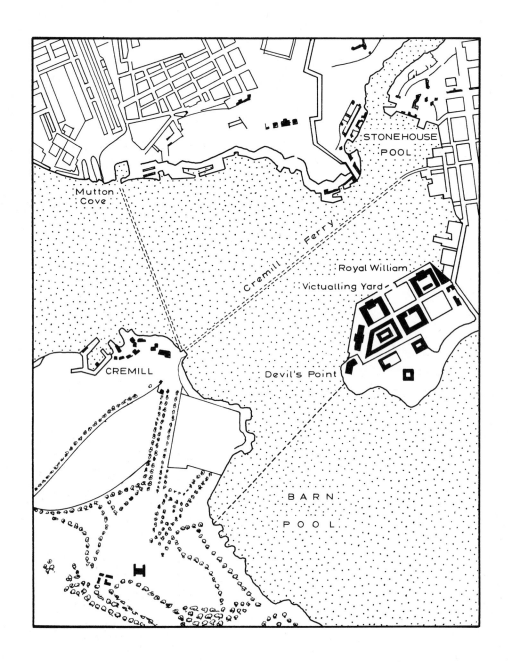

Stonehouse Pool and Cremyll.

ABOVE LEFT: St Andrew's Street, c1880. (S/LS) RIGHT: Looe Street in 1830. (LS) CENTRE: Island House, Barbican, early 1900s. (LS) RIGHT: The Salutation Inn and thirsty workers. (LS) BELOW: Rose and Crown Inn, Old Town Street, early 1900s. (LS)

ABOVE LEFT: The Noah's Ark Inn, c1890. (LS) RIGHT: Watt's Globe Hotel, Bedford Street. (LS) CENTRE LEFT: The Globe Hotel at the junction of Frankfort Street and George Street. (LS) RIGHT: Back of Plymouth Market, 1890s. (LS) BELOW LEFT: The Meat Market RIGHT: East Street Gate to Market.

ABOVE LEFT: The Corn Exchange and Fish Market. (LS) RIGHT: Lower Battery, Citadel, February 1856. (LS) CENTRE: Governor's House, Citadel, 1855. (LS) BELOW: Simplified view of Plymouth in 1821. (LS)

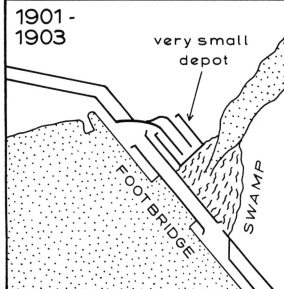

1901 -
1903

very small
depot

FOOTBRIDGE

SWAMP

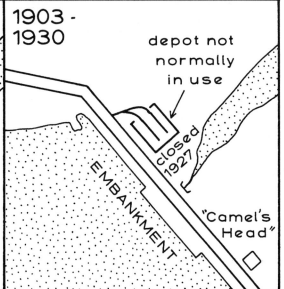

1903 -
1930

depot not
normally
in use

closed
1927

EMBANKMENT

"Camel's
Head"

OPPOSITE ABOVE: Rendel's Iron Bridge. (LS) ABOVE LEFT: Card of the 'new' Torpoint Floating Bridge. (LS) RIGHT: Horse tram, West Hoe. (LS) CENTRE LEFT: Tram on the Peverell route. (LS) RIGHT: Plymouth Corporation tramcar 137, resplendent in new livery. (LS) BELOW: New embankment at Camel's Head improves communications with St Budeaux and Saltash Passage (after Sambourne 1974).

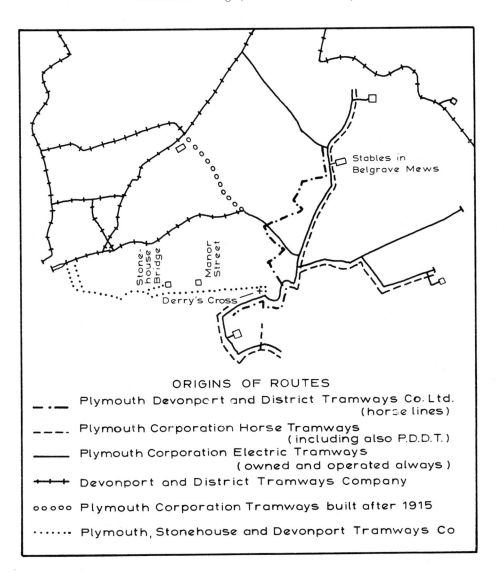

ORIGINS OF ROUTES

—·— Plymouth Devonport and District Tramways Co. Ltd.
(horse lines)

—·—·· Plymouth Corporation Horse Tramways
(including also P.D.D.T.)

——— Plymouth Corporation Electric Tramways
(owned and operated always)

+++ Devonport and District Tramways Company

ooooo Plymouth Corporation Tramways built after 1915

······· Plymouth, Stonehouse and Devonport Tramways Co

Tram routes (after Sambourne 1974).

ABOVE LEFT: Tram approaching Halfpenny Bridge, Stonehouse. (LS)
RIGHT: Baptist Church, Mutley Plain, 1905. (CS) BELOW: Mutley Plain
1905. (CS)

ABOVE: Mutley Plain 1900. (CS) BELOW: Hoe Pier with advertisements,
1903. (CS)

ABOVE: Hoe Pier and yachts in the Sound. (LS) CENTRE: Marine
Biological Association, Laboratory on the Hoe. (CS) LEFT: Cremyll Point,
1900. (CS) RIGHT: Plymouth Guildhall and St Andrew's Church 1903. (CS)

66

F. T. ELLIS, *Licensed to let*
POST HORSES & CARRIAGES
WAGONETES OMNIBUSES DOG CARTS &c
Comfortably fitted for PLEASURE PARTIES *let at*
moderate charges with Single pair
Three or Four Horses. Orders recᵈ Here
or at Sutton road Plyᵗʰ Spring Waggons for
removing furniture in Town & Country. Horses,
Carts & Waggons for Contract and for General Hauling.

ABOVE: Union Street, 1904. (CS) BELOW: Wooden advertising board,
general haulier. (MS)

T. W. BASTOW.

FURNITURE, PLATE, PICTURES, PIANOS, &c.,

PACKED AND REMOVED

TO OR FROM ANY PART OF THE KINGDOM, BY CONTRACT.

LOCK-UP WAREHOUSES. ESTIMATES FREE.

Offices—WESTWELL STREET, PLYMOUTH.

LONDON OFFICES:

For Heavy Goods by Luggage Trains, BELL INN YARD, WARWICK LANE. E.C.

For Parcels and Packages by } AT SUTTON & Co.,
Passenger Trains   } 35, ALDERSGATE STREET. E.C.

Goods and Parcels forwarded Daily from Westwell Street to all parts.

Parcel Delivery Vans to Stonehouse, Devonport, Stoke, and Neighbourhood every Day, (Sundays excepted,) leaving Westwell Street Office at 10 a.m. and 3 p.m.

Parcels, &c., Collected, without extra charge, on notice being sent to the Office.

Small Parcels for Tavistock received up to 8 p.m., delivered by 8 a.m. the following Morning.

All Information as to Rates may be had on application.

AGENT TO THE LIVERPOOL AND LONDON FIRE AND LIFE
ASSURANCE COMPANY.

January, 1862.

PLYMOUTH NURSERY AND SEED ESTABLISHMENT.
DUTCH FLOWER ROOTS.

ALEXANDER PONTEY having received his annual supply of the above, which are unusually fine, begs to offer them at the undermentioned low prices:—

	s. d.	s. d.		s. d.	s. d
Anemones, best named	..	2 0 per doz.	Polyanthus Narcis, named, from 2 6 .. 4 0 per doz.		
" mixed varieties from 0 6 to 0 9			Garden	.. 1 0 .. 2 0 "	
Hyacinths, best named, from .. 0 6 .. 1 0 each.			Jonquils, sweet scented, from .. 1 6 .. 2 0 "		
" mixed, from .. .. 0 4 .. 0 6 "			Snowdrops, from.. .. .. 2 0 .. 2 0 per 100.		
Crocus, best named, from .. 2 0 .. 5 0 per 100.			Iris, mixed and named, from .. 1 0 .. 3 0 per doz.		
" mixed, all colours .. .. 1 8 "			Ixias, splendid varieties, mixed .. 3 0 "		
Tulips, named Early Varieties, 0 0 .. 2 6 per doz.			Sparaxis, fine .. .. 3 0 "		
" Late .. 1 0 .. 3 0 "			Winter Aconites .. .. .. 1 6 "		
Ranunculus, of sorts, from .. 2 0 .. 10 0 per 100.			Gladiolus, named varieties, frm 3 0 .. 4 0 "		

COMPLETE CATALOGUES FREE ON APPLICATION.

Seed Warehouse—21, Cornwall Street. Nurseries—King Street, Plymouth, and Vinstone,
1½ miles from Plymouth, on the Tavistock Road.

THOMAS S. WESTLAKE,

Brass Founder, and Manufacturer of Gas Fittings, Beer Engines, Water Closets, Lift Pumps, Steam Fittings, &c.,

4, FRANKFORT STREET, PLYMOUTH.

Gas Chandeliers, Pillars, Pendants, Brackets, & Fittings of all kinds made to any design.

BRASS FITTINGS FOR DRAPERS' WINDOWS.

ORGAN, FLAT, AND DESK RAILS MADE TO ORDER.

Licensed Victuallers' Bars fitted up on the most approved London style.

PEWTER WORK OF EVERY DESCRIPTION.

ALL KINDS OF BRASS AND GUN METAL, CUT TO PATTERN.

A large Stock of Composition Iron, Brass Tube, & Fittings always on hand, on moderate Terms.

Old Brass Work and Gas Fittings Re-lacquered or Bronzed in a superior manner.

c

ABOVE LEFT: Frankfort Steam Brewery. RIGHT: Mayoral pennant. (MS) BELOW: Advertisements in the 1860s.

ABOVE: Plaque commemorating   improvement in the water supply.
BELOW: Long Bridge, Marsh Mills, 1900. (CS) RIGHT: Plymouth
constable's decorated truncheon. (MS)

ABOVE: Mount Edgcumbe House, 1905. (CS) BELOW: Freedom Park in
the early 20th century. (CS)

THE BEST TREBLE-SCENTED TOILET SOAP "MILL ⊠ BAY."

THE FINEST TRANSPARENT GLYCERINE SOAP, "MILL ⊠ BAY."

MILL ⊠ BAY SOAP.

THE BEST HOUSEHOLD AND TOILET SOAP.

SOLE MAKERS of THE NEW SOAP,

In 12-oz. TABLETS.

Mill ⊠ Bay SELF-WASHER.

The perfection of Laundry Soap. Non-shrinking, highly cleansing, durable in cold or hot water, and entirely free from smell, and from chapping or irritating action on the hands.

May also be used in hot water, but sparingly, as it is stronger and more cleansing than ordinary Soap; and it should not lie soaking in hot water, as thereby much more would be used than is necessary.

"MILL ⊠ BAY" COLD WATER SOAP.

DESIGNED TO SAVE LABOUR, AND THE EXPENSE OF PRODUCING LARGE QUANTITIES OF HOT WATER.

"MILL ⊠ BAY" BATH & TOILET SOAP.

Pure White Crystallized Carbolic Acid, dissolved in Glycerine and Perfume, and added to Pure Soap.

This article differs from ORDINARY COAL TAR SOAP in not containing the Pitch and Dirt of the Tar; but only its active principle, viz.—DISTILLED CARBOLIC ACID, in the form of WHITE CRYSTALS, resembling those of ATTAR OF ROSES. The use of GLYCERINE increases its soothing action on the Skin, while the choice perfume renders it the most agreeable and perfect form of CARBOLIC or "COAL TAR" SOAP yet produced.

ABOVE: 1860s advertisement for the 'famous' Millbay soap. LEFT: Viaduct at Camel's Head settles into the mud. (LS) RIGHT: Farmhouse at Mount Gould before being swallowed up by development. (LS)

ABOVE: Interior of St Andrew's Church. (LS) LEFT: Beaumont Park in the
early 1900s. RIGHT: St Andrew's vicarage in the early 1900s. (LS)

Railways, Docks and Liners

The first local railway was the horse-drawn Plymouth and Dartmoor Railway (P&DR), from Princetown to Marsh Mills, built by Sir Thomas Tyrwhitt as part of his economic plan for Dartmoor. But the plan never took off and the railway was operated by Johnson Brothers, between Foggintor and Swell Tor, to Sutton Pool, solely for the carrying of granite. The success of steam railways, in other parts of England, induced a meeting of prominent businessmen in 1834, in the Plymouth Guildhall, to subscribe money to float the Plymouth, Devonport and Exeter Company. This changed its name to the South Devon and Exeter Company and received its Act in 1844. The line, which had reached Bristol in 1840, was opened to Laira in 1848 and extended to Millbay the following year. The link to Cornwall was provided by the completion of Brunel's Royal Albert Bridge in 1859. This was a tremendous feat of engineering as the foundations had to be laid in 70 feet of water and 20 feet of mud, with strong tidal currents to contend with. Work took place within a 100 feet long, 37 feet diameter iron cylinder from which the water was pumped. This cylinder was moved thirty four times during building, which began in 1849 but was suspended for four years because of financial difficulties. Newspaper accounts report the awe with which huge crowds watched the floating of the first tube in 1857. The tube and rail, carried on pontoons, slid into place without a hitch and was fixed to piers 30 feet above high water. When it was successfully fastened, a band of the Royal Marines struck up and the crowd broke into loud cheers. As the tide receded, the pontoons were removed and the tube rested on the piers, from which it was gradually raised into place by hydraulic pressure. The rail surface of the completed bridge stands 100 feet above the water and the piers, from top to bottom, are 281 feet high. The first locomotive crossed on 11 April 1859 and the bridge was opened on 2 May by the Prince Consort.

By 1876 the Great Western Railway (GWR) had absorbed the local railway companies and the London and South Western Railway (LSWR) had reached Plymouth by running over the GWR line from Lydford to Plymouth, sharing the station at North Road, then running on its own track to a terminus at Devonport. The Plymouth, Devonport and South Western Junction Railway (PDSWJ) opened a line from Lydford to Devonport, with an extension from Bere Alston to Callington. This was leased to and worked by the LSWR but never passed into that company's hands. The LSWR had built, by then, a line from Friary Junction on the GWR line to its new terminus at Friary Station. Competition between the two companies occurred to the east of Plymouth when the LSWR built a railway bridge over the Laira Estuary, beside the Iron Bridge, and constructed a line through Plymstock to Oreston and Turnchapel. The further extension from Plymstock to Yealmpton was eventually won by the GWR.

The development of the docks and dock areas is intimately connected with the coming of the railways. In the 18th century there were three areas worthy of expansion: Sutton Harbour, the Cattewater and Millbay. Piers had been built at Sutton Harbour in 1791 and 1799 but these so cut down the flow of the tide that the Harbour virtually dried out at spring tides. Sir Thomas Tyrwhitt planned to improve the harbour and adapted a plan first put forward in 1786 by

William Simpson, a Duchy of Cornwall surveyor. This involved constructing a wet dock with large dock gates, but a meeting of merchants, traders and shipowners, at the Guildhall, in February 1806, opposed it as it would have meant considerably heavier tolls. However, on 26 June 1811, Royal assent was given to a Sutton Pool Act and in 1812 the Sutton Pool Company was formed with a 99 year lease. The proprietors of this new company met in the Kings Arms, Breton Side, every fortnight. They included the wine merchants Hawker and Collier, Cookworthy, the son of the china clay discoverer, Derry, Lockyer and Sir Michael Seymour. Unfortunately many of their plans for the harbour were thwarted.

Accounts of the time suggest that the harbour was in dire need of discipline and renovation. Robberies were common, pilfering rife and policing inadequate. There were no sheds to protect goods from the weather and the standard of portering was poor. To change this state of affairs a new system of licensing of porters, carmen and draymen was brought in by the Mayor and Justices. Each porter had to provide evidence of good character and had to wear a brass licence plate attached to his arm. Each cart and dray had to be numbered in front by figures not less than three inches in length.

At about this time several prominent men were suggesting ways in which trade could be increased. Edmund Lockyer brought forward a series of propositions on 12 November 1814, which included purchasing vessels to be used in the coal trade from Sunderland and Newcastle and the coal and culm trade to and from Wales. He also urged shipowners to invest in the Baltic trade, in hemp, iron, timber and numerous other products, and trade with the East and West Indies. He reiterated the need for a wet dock, new depots and perhaps the building of a sugar refinery. This suggestion came to fruition in 1852, when the industry was re-established at Coxside, although it proved to be short-lived.

Burt, in his 1816 review of the port of Plymouth, endeavoured to summarize the manufacturers and trade then carried on in the town to encourage greater use of the harbour. The sort of arguments he put forward can be seen in his description of two local brush making firms. The raw materials for these concerns were imported from St Petersburg, Archangel and Koningsberg, first to London and then by coaster to Plymouth. If trade could be established with the Baltic ports, imports could be direct. He suggested that nailmaking, with one concern in Colmer's Lane, could be expanded as could coopering, paper making and iron foundries. At the time Burt was writing there were two local foundries, one of them being Mare's of George Street. This firm later moved to Russell Street, near the Globe Inn, and, among other things, built Hearless Patent Fire Engines and machinery for the 'floating bridge' at Dartmouth. Perhaps Burt's words were heeded, for the number of iron-founders increased to about twenty by the middle of the 19th century.

Trade was certainly growing in the mid-19th century with nearly 400 ships entering the port each year. In 1850 Plymouth was the busiest port in the English Channel and as late as 1860 ranked 6th among all English ports. Sutton Harbour had great hopes that the railway, now pushing steadily westwards, would improve the situation even more. A new company, the Sutton Harbour and Dock Company, was created in 1844, to coordinate activities. The South Devon Railway Company had its own plans for an improved harbour with a wet floating dock designed by Brunel, but these were turned down in 1846 by the Admiralty, because without lock gates the Pool served as a harbour of refuge in times of stormy weather. The railway company then switched its terminus from Eldad to Millbay and partly financed the Great Western Dock Company. The Sutton Harbour and Dock Company was wound up in 1847 and a new concern, the Sutton Harbour Improvement Company, was proposed. This company had high expectations when the LSWR arrived and it bought the harbour from the Duchy of Cornwall in anticipation of being able to make improvements. But the LSWR ran a line from Devonport to Stonehouse Pool and, although a line did get to Sutton Harbour in 1879, a line was also built along the Cattedown waterfront, providing extra competition. Some new quays were added at Sutton and a new fish market was built in 1896 but railway traffic was going elsewhere. Fishing was flourishing, however, and by 1850, sixty trawlers operated from Sutton Harbour. Trade doubled between 1878 and 1888. The first steam trawler appeared in 1896 and, although eagerly awaited, it was the beginning of the decline in the fishing industry as distant fishing grounds were opened up, with operations switching to the east coast ports of Hull, Grimsby and Lowestoft.

Towards the end of the 19th century the Cattewater had increased considerably in importance as a result of the LSWR direct rail link. The building of Batten breakwater and the dredging of the channel also enabled large ships to dock safely. Dock facilities were extended, with Cattedown Wharves built in 1888 and Victoria and Turnchapel Wharf a few years later. Plans by Plymouth Corporation to create a new dock complex were thwarted by the Admiralty in the same way they had blocked the Sutton Harbour development, and also by local merchants, who feared municipalisation. No rational development resulted, yet in 1880 the Cattewater was handling more trade than Sutton Harbour.

A walk around Sutton Harbour and Coxside today reveals many of their developments. The 1820 Customs House and its adjoining warehouses dominate the western arm of the Harbour. The original Customs House, part of an Elizabethan building, stands opposite. The quays were built over a long period of time, with the earliest, Guy's and Vauxhall, existing before 1500. The quays on the western side were replaced when Sutton Wharf was built between 1813 and 1815. North Quay was built by Joseph Lock in 1849-50. Several merchants' houses still exist near the junction of Vauxhall Street and Vauxhall Quay, and Sutton Wharf and North Quay are lined with many 19th century warehouses. The history of Old Teats Hill House, Parr Street, Coxside, reflects well the history of Sutton Harbour. The house is a composite building with the ends considerably older than the middle. It appears that the ends represent two 17th century buildings; a cottage and a rope walk. The present house was the original home of the Westcott family, 18th century shipowners and ship builders, who built their vessels in the creek below the house. Today this creek is bounded by Lockyer and Bayleys Wharves and by Shepherds Quay.

Millbay docks is essentially a creation of the railways but its early days revolve around the deeds of Thomas Gill, son of a Tavistock family who owned quarries, mines and limekilns. He set up a limekiln at Millbay, obtaining limestone from quarries at West Hoe and, in 1818, started an alkali and soap factory which sparked the growth of other chemical industries. A glass factory was built by Stanfords and, in 1823, the United Gas Company set up its works, providing the fuel which was used for the first street lighting in 1832. William Bryant, another industrialist, had starting making starch and refining sugar on a site at Millbay in 1838, and then joined with Francis May to make matches. Unfortunately they burnt down the factory in the process, moved to London to begin again and started the Swan Vesta Company.

Gill's continued efforts led to the Millbay Soap, Alkali and Soda Company in 1856. Meanwhile he became Mayor in 1836 and was Liberal MP between 1841-6. He also saw the possibilities of a new dock complex at Millbay and built a 500 feet long pier in 1844, at a cost of £27,000, which allowed ships of 3,000 ton to dock. Brunel's *Great Britain* used the pier on her trial voyage in 1845. Gill also became chairman of the South Devon Railway Company, which built its terminus at Millbay, after the Sutton Harbour plans were vetoed by the Admiralty. A new Great Western Dock Company was then formed to develop the docks to Brunel's design and by 1850 there were a railway link, Customs House, and Pier Hotel, and the dock had been recognised as a Government mail packet station. The GWR became sole owner in 1874 and improved the facilities by adding the deep West Wharf.

Plymouth had always been well placed for passenger traffic, whether to North America or to the developing countries of the east. The Channel Isles were also close, and in 1822 the

Plymouth and Portsmouth Steam Packet Company was formed, operating two steamers, the *Sir Francis Drake* and the *Brunswick*. The *Sir Francis Drake* had been built at Cattedown as a schooner and was converted to steam in the same yard. The service operated between Falmouth, Portsmouth and the Channel Isles. The building of the Millbay complex opened up prospects of international services and in 1850 the town celebrated the departure of the first Cape mails in the *Bosphorous*. Plymouth became the Australian mail port in 1852 and all the large British companies called regularly. Plymouth was essentially a port of call on the way to London, Southampton or Liverpool and as liners got bigger they had to anchor in the Sound. Tenders ferried mail and passengers to Millbay and, by 1890, five tenders, named after Elizabethan sea-captains, were operating. These were kept busy as European liners, (especially French and German), began to use Plymouth on their Atlantic runs. P and O increased their use of the port and White Star and Holland-America followed. Until 1882, passengers had to be taken to Millbay Station in cabs, but facilities were gradually improved and then boat trains could start from the dockside. Early in the 20th century more than 500 liners called each year and in 1913 more than 30,000 passengers passed through Millbay. A rival terminus, Ocean Quay, was built in 1904 under Mount Wise by the LSWR at the end of its Stonehouse Pool line. The GWR, in retaliation, started a service to Brest as competition to the LSWR Southampton-Le Harvre service. This competition ceased in 1910 when the LSWR abandoned its liner quay and the GWR stopped the Brest service.

A number of other developments had taken place at Millbay. In 1828, the Royal Union Baths had been opened, in which sea water was brought in iron pipes from Rusty Anchor and mixed with magnesium and lime salts from a mineral spring. The buildings comprised two swimming baths, six plunge and nine hot baths and was a social and remedial centre. These baths were removed during the subsequent development of Millbay. The growth of the liner traffic led to the building of three large hotels. The Duke of Cornwall was built in 1862, followed by the Albion, which became the Albion and Continental when it took over the Royal Eye Infirmary premises in 1904. Finally, the Grand Hotel was built on the Hoe in 1880.

The position of Plymouth also led to its adoption as a major emigration depôt. The founder of the New Zealand Company, Edward Wakefield, had sailed from Sutton Harbour on 12 May 1839 in the *Torry* with a party of settlers. The following year the Plymouth Company of New Zealand was formed, and six ships, with 897 settlers, set out to establish New Plymouth on the North Island, New Zealand. Most emigration was to North America, and the Colonial Land and Emigration Commissions were set up in 1840 to direct emigration to South Africa, New Zealand and Australia. Plymouth was chosen as one of the depôts where emigrants waited for chartered ships, and a depôt was set up in the vacated victualling yard premises near Fisher's Nose. This had over 1,000 berths by 1883 and, when assisted passage ended at the beginning of the 20th century, over 300,000 emigrants had sailed from Plymouth.

The Dockyard, as well as the commercial ports, continued to grow and was boosted by the Crimean War. This was also the period when the first ironclad ships with screw propellers began to replace paddle steamers, which had always been vulnerable to attack. The change in ship types required a change in dock facility and so the Keyham steam factory was started in 1844 and completed in 1854. It consisted of two basins, three graving docks and a tunnel under high land behind the Gun Wharf to link the two yards. The GWR line passes through Keyham, one hundred yards from the Dockyard wall and was linked, through the tunnel, with the yards. Until this link with the railway, huge traction engines called 'camels' had been used to bring in materials. By 1890 the dockyard was again too small and the mouth of Camel's Head Creek was developed with a modern tidal basin, closed basin and graving docks. Much material for this construction was dredged from Start Bay, off Hallsands, and is thought to have played a part in the destruction of that village by storms.

The Dockyard was an integral part of the nation's defences and the antics of Napoleon III persuaded the Palmerston Government that its naval ports should be protected. Twenty nine forts and batteries were built around Plymouth and on the shores of the Sound. Many of these are now overgrown but a number have been adapted to other purposes, such as Bovisand and Picklecombe forts. New barracks were also built; one at Mutley in 1840 and the Raglan Barracks in 1854. The forts, when constructed, were on the edge of the town, but many were soon to be engulfed as the town spread outwards.

The Dockyard played a prominent role in the development of the big battleships. The designer of the King Edward VII class battleships was Sir William White, a Devonport man who began his career as a boy in the Dockyard. In March 1902, King Edward and Queen Alexandra visited Devonport to launch the battleship *HMS Queen* and to lay the keel plate of the *King Edward VII*. To honour the occasion the Corporation presented them with a silver casket surmounted by a model of the *Golden Hind*. *The King Edward VII* was launched on 23 July 1903 by the Prince and Princess of Wales. Admiral, Prince Louis of Battenburg was also present at the launch. These battleships, and many others built at Devonport, were to play a major role in the great sea-battles of the First World War. The town then had to face the feverish activity it had always experienced when the nation went to war.

ABOVE: Early construction of Brunel's Royal Albert Bridge. (LS) BELOW: Floating of one section of Brunel's Royal Albert Bridge. (LS)

ABOVE: Royal Albert Bridge. (CS) BELOW: Brunel's wooden bridge at
Pennycomequick. (LS)

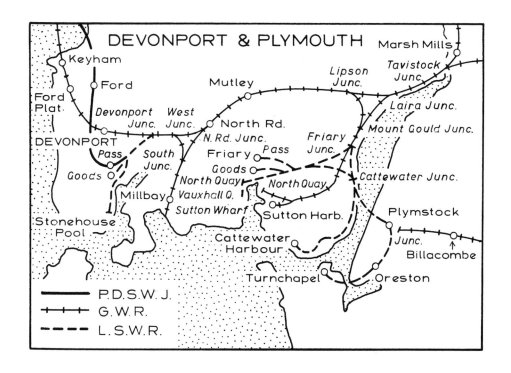

ABOVE: Railway layout of Plymouth in the early 20th century. BELOW:
Railways come to Sutton Harbour.

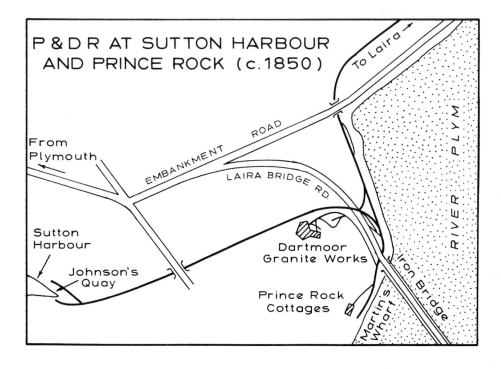

LEFT AND BELOW: Sutton Harbour in the 1860s. (LS) RIGHT: Sutton
Harbour and Customs House, 1850. (LS)

LEFT: Warehouse at Sutton Harbour. RIGHT: Barbican fish market, c1890. (LS) CENTRE: Barbican Fish Quay. (LS) BELOW: Extension to the Dockyard at Keyham in the late 19th century. (LS)

ABOVE: North extension of Dockyard, 1905. (LS) BELOW: The Hamoaze
from Millbrook, 1903. (CS)

ABOVE: Saltash and ships, 1904. (CS) LEFT: The *Yvonne* thrown onto the breakwater in a storm. (LS) RIGHT: Channel Fleet in the Sound, late 19th century. (LS) CENTRE: Result of the Christmas hurricane, 1912. (LS) BELOW: HMS *Captain* and *Agincourt* in the Sound. (LS)

LEFT: Plymouth, Turnchapel and Oreston Ferry at Turnchapel.
(LS) BELOW: Steamers at Phoenix Wharf, 1905. (CS) RIGHT: Millbrook
steamer *Empress*. (LS)

ABOVE LEFT: Millbrook steamers on a pleasure outing. (LS) RIGHT and
BELOW LEFT: Steamer *Britannia*. (LS) CENTRE: Picklecombe, one of the
19th century fortifications. (CS) BELOW RIGHT: Commemoration of the
departure of the *Tory* for New Zealand.

ABOVE: Mount Wise, Devonport, 1905. (CS) BELOW: Yachts in the
Sound, 1905. (CS)

Days of War and Peace

Plymouth was never threatened directly in the First World War, but the Dockyard was kept extremely busy and the army barracks were scenes of great activity. But Plymouth and Plymothians were deeply affected indirectly in the mounting casualty lists at sea and on land. All the major sea-battles involved Devonport ships and local men and, in France, regiments such as the 2nd Devons were in the front line. The threat of invasion might have been slight but the War Office put into operation a precautionary defence scheme. It was generally thought that the sea approaches to Plymouth were virtually impregnable; the eastern approach was closed by a boom and nets and the western entrance was heavily guarded. At first, a guard was placed on railway bridges and viaducts and road blocks were set up on all main roads leading to Plymouth, as precautions against spies and saboteurs. But the town suffered little inconvenience, the sea approaches were never troubled and ships passed in and out of the Sound unmolested.

The unexpected arrival of the Canadian Expeditionary Force, on 14 October 1914, aroused great interest. The convoy consisted of thirty three liners with 25,000 men and had originally planned to dock at Southampton, but was diverted to Plymouth because of German submarine activity in the Channel. As the war progressed, news of sea-battles filtered back to the naval ports. Three cruisers *Aboukir*, *Hogue* and *Cresey* were sunk by a submarine off the Dutch coast and the battleship *Audacious* was lost on 27 October 1914. The biggest early disaster for the town was the loss of the *Monmouth* and *Good Hope*, in the Battle of Coronel in the South Pacific, against Admiral Von Spee. The *Monmouth* had been a Devonport-manned ship. A few days later the dreadnought cruisers *Invincible* and *Inflexible* arrived at Devonport to be fitted out, in record time, to take part in the Battle of the Falkland Islands. In this operation, Admiral Sturdee, in charge of the fleet, surprised and destroyed the *Scharnhorst*, *Gneisenau*, *Nurnberg* and *Leipzig*, virtually the whole of Von Spee's Squadron.

The Battle of Jutland, in May 1916, was a great blow to the town. The Royal Navy lost fourteen ships, many Devonport-manned, and 6,274 men. One of the ships involved in that battle was the 26,000 ton battle cruiser *Lion*, flagship of the Vice-Admiral Sir David Beatty. She was a Devonport-built ship and manned by Devonport men. The ship was badly damaged but was saved from destruction by the heroic action of a turret officer, Major F. J. W. Harvey, who ordered a magazine to be flooded, for which action he was awarded a posthumous Victoria Cross. Other Devonport-built ships involved at Jutland included the *Minotaur*, *Temeraire*, *Collingwood*, *Indefatigable* sunk with only two survivors, *Centurion* and *Marlborough* which limped back to the Humber after being torpedoed. The names of the military Personnel killed in action are remembered on the War Memorial erected after the war on the Hoe.

The Dockyard was kept busy repairing damaged ships but also managed to build and lay down new ships. The most famous was the 27,500 ton battleship *Royal Oak* which was launched in November 1914 and commissioned 1 May 1916 to form one of the Fourth Battle Squadron at Jutland. The ship survived all the vicissitudes of the First World War and lasted until the opening skirmishes of the Second World War. The Dockyard was also producing J & K class submarines. The K class vessels possessed the unusual feature of two funnels, giving them a surface speed of 24 knots and enabling them to keep up with the fleet. Unfortunately one of them, K6, refused to surface the first time she was submerged in a non-tidal basin in the Dockyard, much to the consternation of the Yard employees. The fault was repaired by L. Selley, Inspector of Engine Fitters, who was later awarded the OBE.

The latter years of the war will be remembered for the presence of the Americans and the 'Q' ship activities. The Americans took over Victoria Wharf as a base in June 1917 and operated a large number of Henry Ford's mass-produced submarine chasers. 'Q' ships were decoy ships made to look like innocent tramp vessels. When challenged by a U-boat, the officers and crew, behaving as would be expected, abandoned ship. The U-boat would eventually come closer and then the fake bulwarks of the 'Q' ship would fall away, the White Ensign run up and the U-boat would be attacked with the revealed ship's guns. Many 'Q' ships operated from Devonport but their activities were closely guarded secrets.

The major problem that faced the town after the war was the provision of new housing. New housing estates were started at North Prospect and Swilly and, by 1924, 802 new houses had been built. The Corporation housing programme developed steadily and, in addition, the GWR built an estate at Peverell and the Astors another at Mount Gould. The admiralty also began building houses at St Budeaux. The town had now grown to its official boundaries and land for future development was limited. The population of the inner areas was declining but the outer suburbs, especially Plympton and Plymstock, were growing rapidly. Plymstock grew from 7,032 in 1901 to 12,134 in 1931. Plymouth eventually gained a boundary extension in 1938, but Plymstock and Plympton were still outside the Plymouth limit.

The expanding town needed an expanded transport system. The Corporation centralised its garaging at the Milehouse depot and bought its first 'buses in 1920 to serve places remote from the tram network. The 'buses gradually replaced the trams and in 1939 the Peverell route was the only one still operated by tramcars. Private 'bus companies were set up just after the war, using 'buses rebuilt on army lorry chasses. The first major private firm was the Embankment Motor Company, followed by the Devon Motor Transport Company. There was stiff competition and considerable fare cutting between these firms until the Devon Motor Transport Company was taken over by the National Bus Company, which operated the first double-deck 'buses. In 1929 the GWR acquired a controlling interest in road transport and formed the Western National Omnibus Company.

The post-war cut back in employment and the depression years caused a change in the political framework. Parliamentary reorganisation in 1918 had reduced Plymouth to three Members of Parliament for the constituencies of Devonport, Sutton and Drake. Waldorf Astor, who had been MP from 1910, succeeded to his father's title in 1919. This meant a by-election for the Sutton constituency, which his wife Nancy fought and won with a majority of five thousand. It was, by all accounts, a keenly contested seat and the result was in doubt right up to the end. Nancy Astor was the first woman MP to take her seat in the House of Commons.

The General Strike of 1926 affected Plymouth as much as any city. The Dockyard had been laying-off men for a number of years and unemployment was becoming a problem. Plymouth had always relied too much on the Dockyard and when the Dockyard 'caught a cold' the whole town 'sneezed'. It was in this context that allegiance to the Labour Party grew with J. J. H. (Jimmy) Moses, leader of the Shipwrights' Union, as prime mover. By 1923 Jimmy Moses was an Alderman and in 1926 was elected as Plymouth's first Labour Mayor. The General Election of 1929 resulted in weeks of hectic activity and a series of frantic hustings. Large crowds gathered outside the Guildhall as the results were announced. It soon became clear that Hore-Belisha had held Devonport for the Liberals and that Jimmy Moses had won Drake to become Plymouth's first Labour MP. The result of the Sutton constituency was extremely close, with Nancy Astor winning after a recount.

A year before, in 1928, the Borough had been granted the privileges and title of a City by King George V and a tablet to commemorate the event was placed in the northern wall of the Guildhall. In 1935, the City received its second charter from the King when it was granted the right to use the style of Lord Mayor. This was given to the City in celebration of the Silver Jubilee.

In the inter-war years Plymouth became a major entertainment and shopping centre for the whole of Devon and Cornwall. Major stores, such as Spooner's, Popham's, Yeo's and Dingle's, were consolidating their custom in Plymouth, whereas Devonport's shopping centre was declining. Many excursions from all parts of the West Country combined a shopping trip with an afternoon watching Plymouth Argyle Football Club. The Club has started in the Southern League, along with teams like West Ham United and Tottenham Hotspur, but in the 1920s and 1930s, when the team was going up and down between the Third and Second Divisions of the Football League, it drew good crowds. Central Park by then had come into existence as a park because of the Bath and West Show, which was scheduled in 1922 at Home Park. Hurried preparations were made for this show, such as widening Alma Road to Milehouse and the laying of a new tram track.

The City was well served by cinemas and theatres. The Hoe Pier was the home of touring concert parties and people strolling along the promenade on a summer's evening would hear the sounds of singing and dancing carried on the sea-breezes. At the turn of the century the Palace Theatre of Varieties, the Royal and Grand Theatre, had packed houses, but in the 1920s cinemas had captured most of their audiences. A picture house was built in Union Street, then the Cinedrome in Ebrington Street was turned into the New Palladium and the Regent and Gaumont cinemas built. In 1938 the Royal Theatre was replaced by a 2,400 seater cinema.

Plymouth had achieved its status as a city and was gradually increasing in size and in the facilities it offered the surrounding region. Employment in the Dockyard was rising but the City, during the 1930's, still had an above average unemployment rate. The liner trade was still thriving with 30-40,000 passengers annually passing through the port, together with an enormous number of mail bags. The famous Cunard liners, *Aquitania*, *Mauretania* and *Queen Mary* were frequent visitors. Fish harvests were generally good and boats working out of Sutton Harbour did well. But the political situation was changing and the German threat instigated a re-armament programme and the rapid build-up of the Dockyard. Nobody could have foreseen the dramatic events that were to overtake Plymouth after 1939.

HMS *Hood*. (LS)

LEFT: The *Queen Mary* entering the Sound in the 1930s. (LS) RIGHT: The *Devonia* at Millbay. (LS) BELOW: Post Office and Guildhall Square, 1929. (CS)

ABOVE LEFT: Rescue from the floods at Forder Valley. (LS) RIGHT: Mopping up after the Forder Valley floods. (LS) BELOW: Bar of the Royal Hotel. (LS)

LEFT: Palm Court of the Royal Hotel. (LS) RIGHT: High Street entrance to Nicholls Court. (LS) BELOW: Frankfort Street and Coster's Store in the 1930s. (LS)

43382
STONEHOUSE
BRIDGE

Foot Passenger
1d
2
Not Transferable

RETURN SAME DAY
This Ticket must
be given up on
Return or Toll paid

Williamson, Printer, Ashton.

Dedicated to the Freedom of the Plymouth Toll Gates, Tuesday, April 1st, 1924.

In Loving Memory

OF THE

HALF=PENNY GATE

whose career was finished by the

Mayor & Corporation in State.

After the years I've bled you
   Of half-pennies to pass my way,
Its no wonder you are all smiling
   Over my demise to-day.
I've took toll of your Grandfather's
   Grandfather,
Your Grandmother's Grandmother too,
And also their great great grandparents
   As well as taking it from you.
I'd have taken it from your children's
   children,
   And also their children as well
If I had only been allowed to go on
   Instead of being consigned to— finis.
Composed by " Red."

Now we pay no longer,
   From to-day its free,
No more will you pay for the pleasure
   Of walking over me.
I should have been " done in "
   Five score years ago,
For a town the size of Plymouth
   My finish has been very slow.

LEFT: Pennycomequick toll gate. (LS) RIGHT: Last toll ticket at Stonehouse Bridge on the day tolls were abolished. (MS) BELOW: Ode to the last toll gates. (MS)

• GREAT WESTERN RAILWAY.

CAB FARES

For HORSE DRIVEN VEHICLES between the

PLYMOUTH (NORTH ROAD) RAILWAY STATION STAND

AND

	s.	d.		s.	d.
Admiral's Hard, Stonehouse	1	4	Marine Barracks, Stonehouse	1	4
Admiral's House, Mount Wise	1	8	Mechanics Institute, Plymouth	–	8
Alma Villas, Saltash Road		8	Millbay Railway Station	1	0
Albert Road, Morice Town, Coach Stand	1	4	Mount Wise Barracks	1	8
"Albion" Hotel	1	0			
Barbican Coach Stand	1	0	Naval Hospital Gate	1	0
Belmont Place, Coach Stand, Stoke	1	0	North Corner, Devonport	1	8
Charles Church		8	Oreston Ferry	1	8
Charles Place, West End of	1	0	Osborne Villas, Stoke Road, Junction at	–	8
Cattedown Manure Works	1	4	"Outlands House," First Mile Post near	1	0
Coxside, Junction of Roads at Clare Place	1	4			
Citadel Gate	1	0	Penlee Villas, Stoke (to Gate only)		8
Customs House	0	8	Powder Magazine, Gate of Road to	1	8
Conservative Club House		8	Post Office, Plymouth	–	8
			Post Office, Devonport	1	4
Dockyard Gate, Devonport	1	8	Prison Gate, Plymouth	1	0
Devonport G.W. Railway Station Coach Stand.	1	0	Prudential Buildings	–	8
Devonport L. & S.W. Railway Coach Stand	1	0			
Duke Street, Devonport, Coach Stand	1	8	Raglan Barracks, Devonport	1	8
"Duke of Cornwall" Hotel	1	0	Roman Catholic Cathedral		8
Elphinstone Barracks Gate	1	0	"Royal" Hotel, Plymouth		8
Embankment Road, Turnpike	1	4	"Royal" Hotel, Devonport	1	4
Efford, Junction of Roads to	1	4	Richmond Walk, Baths at	1	8
"Farley" Hotel, Union Street		8	Royal Albert Hospital	1	0
Fore Street Coach Stand, Devonport	1	8	Royal Western Yacht Club	1	0
Granby Barracks, Devonport	1	4	Sisters of Mercy House at Plymouth		8
"Grand" Hotel	1	0	"Stert" House, First Mile Post at	1	4
Gunwharf Gate	1	8	St. George's Hall, Stonehouse	1	4
Government House, Mount Wise	1	8	Stoke Parish Church	1	0
Guildhall, Devonport	1	8	"Swilley House" Gate, First Mile Post near	1	0
Guildhall, Plymouth		8			
"Great Western" Hotel, Plymouth (NEAR PALACE THEATRE)	1	0	Temperance Hall, Devonport	1	4
Halfpenny Gate	1	4	Townsend Hill, Mutley, First Mile Post on	1	0
Keyham Turnpike	1	8	Torpoint Ferry Coach Stand	1	4
Keyham Official Residences	1	4	Torpoint Ferry Lamp Post	1	8
			Torpoint Ferry Gate at Torpoint	2	0
Laira Green, Second Mile Post from Plymouth	1	8	"Thomas'" Hotel, Devonport	1	4
Lipson Terrace, First Mile Post near	1	0			
Liberal Club House		8	Waterloo Street, Devonport, Coach Stand	1	0
"Lockyer" Hotel, Lockyer Street		8	West Hoe Terrace	1	0
Millbay Pier Hotel	1	0	Winter Villa, North Gate	1	8
Manor Office, Chapel Street, Devonport	1	8	"Westminster" Hotel		8
			Yealmpton Road, First Mile Post on	1	4

BYE-LAWS FOR REGULATING

HACKNEY COACHES, FLYS, & OTHER CARRIAGES.

TIME. For Carriages drawn by One Horse. For any time not exceeding half an hour, 1 6 ; for any time not exceeding one hour 2 6 ; for every additional quarter of an hour, or fractional part thereof, 6d. The hirer may pay by time instead of by distance, provided he states his intention of doing so at the time of hiring. When the carriage is hired by time, the driver may be required to drive at the rate of four miles an hour ; should he be required to exceed that rate, then he shall be entitled to demand an addition to the fare regulated by time, the rate by distance for every mile or part thereof (not completed) exceeding four miles. When more than two persons are taken in any carriage one sum of 6d. is to be paid for each person above the number of two, for the whole hiring, in addition to the fare by distance for two persons. No passengers to be allowed for carriages drawn by more than one horse, unless the parties shall have agreed on a fare previously to the hiring.

WAITING TIME. When a carriage is hired by distance, the hirer may detain the same in waiting free of extra charge for any period not exceeding altogether during the hiring ten minutes, but the driver of every carriage so engaged shall, after the expiration of such last-mentioned ten minutes, be entitled to the sum of 6d. for every quarter of an hour, or fractional part thereof, as a waiting time fare.

DAY FARES.—Distance for Carriages drawn by One Horse. For one or two adults, any distance not exceeding one mile, 8d ; for every fractional part of a half mile, 4d. Not more than the following number of persons, in addition to the driver, can be carried in each carriage respectively : Four adults inside and one outside a four-wheeled carriage drawn by one horse ; two adults inside a two-wheeled carriage drawn by one horse. For the purpose aforesaid, children under three years of age not to be charged for, from three to twelve to be charged half fare, whether by time or distance, and two children from three to twelve years of age, to be considered as one adult. The mileage commences from the point of hiring.

LUGGAGE. The hirer shall be at liberty to take any quantity of luggage which can conveniently and without injury to the carriage be placed within the same free of charge ; but for every package taken outside the carriage, the driver shall be entitled to 2d.

The driver of every carriage shall, without demanding or receiving any extra payment therefore, assist in loading or unloading luggage, and in conveying the same to or from the inside door of the house or place at which he may be taking up or setting down a fare.

NIGHT. For as much of the hiring as shall take place between the hours of half-past eleven p.m. and half-past five a.m., the fare, with the exception of what shall be chargeable on account of luggage, shall be double the day or ordinary fare.

TOLLS. All tolls must be paid by the hirer.

The driver of any carriage may refuse to take any dog or other animal in or upon his carriage. The driver of any carriage must, on being desired by the hirer, immediately proceed to the place directed by him, the amount of the fare being first paid the driver, if demanded. Private bargains between the hirer and driver may be made either for time or distance, but if for more than the fare, the same cannot be enforced.

PADDINGTON, May, 1916.
P - 3332.   32 100

FRANK POTTER, General Manager.

N 7696

Latimer, Trend & Co. Printers, 165, Union Street, Plymouth.

Horse cab fares from North Road Station, 1916. (MS)

ABOVE: Western National Leyland 'bus recalled for service. (LS) CENTRE LEFT: Bedford Street before the blitz. (CS) RIGHT: Union Street before the blitz. (CS) BELOW LEFT: Saltash Bridge and steam ferry boats, 1920. RIGHT: Water front at Oreston. (LS)

ABOVE: First bomb to fall, Swilly. (LS) BELOW: Damage at the Meat
Market. (LS)

The Blitz

When war was declared, local reaction was mixed. It meant new employment in armament programmes, a full dockyard and servicemen to spend their money in the City, but some emergency measures were instituted and, from September 1939, Plymouth rehearsed methods of dealing with attack from the air. Anti-aircraft batteries were established, barrage balloons developed and air raid sirens were put under single remote control at Greenbank Police Headquarters. The 'phoney war' dragged on with life continuing much as before and it was not until the Germans had reached the English Channel in France, in the summer of 1940, that Plymouth began to consider its vulnerability. As a major Naval Dockyard it was always going to be a significant target, but most people thought the war would not last more than a few months.

The early period of the war was enlivened by the return of the ships *Ajax* and *Exeter* after their successful action against the pocket battleship *Graf Spee* in the River Plate, Argentina. The *Ajax* slipped into the Sound unnoticed on 30 January, 1940 and, when news leaked out, was given a rapturous welcome. The return of the *Exeter*, on 15 February, was even more enthusiastically received. She was extensively damaged but had been 'patched up' *en route* to appear less vulnerable. The *Exeter* had been built in Devonport and many of the crew were local. The ship and crew were welcomed by Sir Winston Churchill, the First Lord of the Admiralty, who joined the ship in the Hamoaze before she docked. Other members of the visiting party were Admiral of the Fleet Sir Dudley Pound, the First Sea Lord and Sir John Simon, Chancellor of the Exchequer. The *Exeter*, after a lengthy refit in Devonport, joined the First Cruiser Squadron in the Home Fleet, and later worked in the Middle East. On 1 March 1942, she was scuttled by her crew after valiant action against overwhelming Japanese forces in the Dutch East Indies. During this action 54 officers and men were lost.

The pace of events was speeding up and in the middle of June 1940, 70-80,000 French troops, who had been evacuated from Dunkirk, were re-embarked at Millbay Docks. The first real impact of the war was felt by the City in the next few months. The first siren alarm sounded on 30 June and the population grudgingly made their way to the nearest shelter. This happened to be a false alarm but during the next four years the sirens were to sound over four hundred times and there were to be 59 bombing raids. The first of these raids occurred just before midday on 6 July 1940, when a single 'plane dropped the first bomb in Swilly Road, Devonport. Three houses were destroyed, two others wrecked and one man, one woman and a boy killed. Six other people were injured. Even after the first raid and these first casualties there was no consideration of evacuation and, paradoxically, children from London and the big cities of the Midlands were being evacuated to Plymouth as the bombs were falling.

The next raid occurred late in the afternoon of the following day, a Sunday. 'Planes flew down the Plym Valley and Home Sweet Home Terrace, in Cattedown was hit, killing six people. The third attack, the next morning, hit Devonport, especially Morice Square. One bomb fell straight through the Royal Sailors Club but miraculously nobody was hurt. Two days later Exeter Street and the Hoe District were hit, killing five people. The pattern of small raids continued for the next few weeks and it appears that selective targets were chosen such as RAF Mount Batten, the Dockyard, and public utilities, such as the gas and electricity works, and North Road Station. The highest fatalities occurred when a bomb hit a queue waiting outside a fish and chip shop at the corner of Chapel Street and Emma Place in Stonehouse. Thirteen were killed and fifteen injured, five seriously.

Air defences were virtually non-existent and it was possible to stand on the Hoe and watch, in broad daylight, German bombers attacking the City and ships anchored in the Sound. Some protection was provided by the guns of the cruiser *Newcastle*, moored in the Sound. Even after these extensive raids Plymouth was not made an evacuation area; that was not to happen until well into 1941. Many families, however, left the city for the safer towns and villages of Devon and Cornwall. This evacuation, at first unofficial but later official, was to reduce the population of the City by half by the end of the war. Early confusion was substantial, with a lack of direction and misunderstanding over positions of responsibility. Arrangements for emergency feeding and housing were, at first, unsatisfactory as many of the premises used for these purposes were close to target areas and were repeatedly hit, meaning new premises had to be found. There was also remarkably little help from Whitehall, and the powers in London seemed reluctant even to acknowledge that Plymouth faced potential destruction. Local government was made difficult by the loss of records and the repeated destruction of offices. Council Offices were eventually dispersed throughout Plymouth, Stonehouse and Devonport. Enlistment caused further problems by depleting the number of civic employees. Early protection facilities for the general public were scanty and many of the early shelters were small and easily flooded. Anderson shelters were free to households with an income less that £250 per annum, and later on Morrison shelters became available.

The Lord Mayor in 1939 was G. S. Scoble but he was replaced on 9 November by Lord Astor, who served in that capacity for the duration of the war. While Lord Astor worked continuously within the City, Lady Astor battled nationally to obtain recognition for Plymouth's plight. She was most scathing when, in May 1941, the House of Commons debated the Fire Services (Emergency Provisions) Bill, after Plymouth had suffered over six months of blitz and fire.

The pattern of the blitz changed in the last months of 1940. The bombs gradually increased in size and some were over a ton in weight. New land mines were dropped by parachute but the major change was the use of incendiaries. The first incendiary attack came on 28 November 1940 when several thousand were dropped, together with a hundred tons of bombs. Mount Batten was extensively damaged when hangers and oil tanks were hit. A Sunderland flying boat, moored in the Cattewater, also suffered a direct hit. It has been estimated that a hundred 'planes took part in the raid and fires were raging in a zone from the Barbican east to Plymstock and north to Crownhill. The first incendiaries were small and could be tackled with water and sand by individuals but later, explosive and non-explosive types were mixed with delayed firing devices that burnt while being tackled. During one attack, both the Plymouth and Stonehouse Gas Company and the Plymouth Corporation Electricity Works were hit and the City was without power. Local gas supplies were constantly disrupted and many tragic accidents occurred during repair work. The incendiaries destroyed hundreds of houses and the Emergency Committee, set up to run the City during the war, was faced with the task of feeding and housing the homeless. The Council provided food and shelter for two days, and after that people were billeted in private houses with an allowance of 5s for each adult and 3s for each child to the hosts.

A welcome respite, on 20 March 1941, was provided by the visit of the King and Queen, together with the Australian Prime Minister, Robert Menzies. The King inspected Civil Defence and Home Guard units and talked to many local people before departing in the Royal Train from Millbay. But only hours after the Royal Train had left the City, the heaviest air raid so far encountered began. The first wave of attack consisted of thousands of incendiaries. Spooner's store at St Andrew's Cross burst into flames, as did the Royal Hotel. The illumination provided by these fires enabled the second wave of 'planes to bomb the whole town from Stonehouse to Mutley and Cattedown. The centre was extensively damaged, including St Andrew's Church, and in that one night 336 people were killed. The damage inflicted on the following night, 21 March, was even more extensive. The heat was so intense from the fires that plate glass melted and asphalt roadways turned to liquid. The Guildhall was hit, St Andrew's Church further damaged and the large Cooperative store mostly destroyed, but Derry's Clock somewhat amazingly survived. A bomb at the Royal Naval Barracks destroyed a petty officers' block, killing eighty men, a large underground shelter in Portland Square suffered a direct hit and seventy two people died. Milehouse 'bus depot was virtually obliterated and one complete 'bus was thrown onto the roof of the main shed. Fifty 'buses were destroyed. Many churches were burnt out, such as King Street Wesleyan Church and the Baptist Church in George Street. Charles Church remains to this day as a memorial to those events. The Hoe Pier, Hoe Cafe and Hoe Grammar School were bombed along with the Prince of Wales Hospital. The Royal Sailors Rest was also destroyed. Further raids occurred in April, bringing the death toll in March and April 1941 to 926. In one of these raids the Astor's house at 3 Elliot Terrace was damaged.

Newspaper accounts of the time recall the horror of the raids and the bravery of many individuals. The *Western Evening Herald* of Friday 21 March reported a number of babies born during the height of the blitz. On a lighter note a barmaid recalled how she was pouring out the lemon for the shandy a customer had ordered when there was an 'awful bang' and the place shook. She dropped the bottle and glass but the customer got his shandy before they had to leave the pub. A girl from Carlisle recounts being in a cinema when it was hit, being directed to another building but which was on fire and then having to walk five miles home, only to fall into a bomb crater within sight of home. The newspaper reports also show the sadder side of the war. Looting of bombed premises was common and some houses were repeatedly looted. Some owners of property in the countryside around Plymouth were quick to exploit the situation, and charged exorbitant rent to evacuees. Families who trekked to the edge of Dartmoor each night were even charged rent for sleeping in cowsheds.

It is interesting to note the contrast in official communiques, largely for security reasons on the British side, and for propaganda on the German side, that were put out concerning these raids. Of the raid on the night of 20/21 March, 1941, the Air Ministry of Home Security statement read:

'Enemy activity last night was on a much smaller scale than of late and was divided between a town in the South-West of England and London. In the former, the attack, though not of long duration, succeeded in starting a number of fires. Damage was also done by high explosive bombs in a number of parts of the town but reports so far received do not indicate that casualties will be heavy'.

According to the German News Agency, the explosives caused many fires which looked like a sea of flame over a large area. In the harbour a large naval supply depôt was completely destroyed by fire. 'It can be stated that the damage caused in the harbour of Plymouth and on works of military importance in the rest of the town was extremely serious . . .'

Although the City was extensively damaged, great efforts were made to restore some semblance of normality. Most of the big stores, such as Dingle's, Spooner's Yeo's and Popham's, moved to smaller shops on the edge of the centre and many open air stalls were erected. Mutley Plain had escaped damage and became the major shopping area. After the raid on Monday 28 April, A. Titherley, Senior Regional Officer of the Ministry of Health, met the City's Emergency Committee and fianally agreed that a large part of Plymouth should be declared an evacuation area, but only certain areas were to be scheduled for evacuation in the first instance. For several weeks prior to this local officials had operated an evening evacuation. A few weeks later Churchill visited the area. Lord Astor was ill and he was met and entertained by Nancy Astor. Morale was lifted, albeit temporarily, but no lasting improvement materialised and little help came from the National Government.

Daily life became extremely difficult. Plymouth was a protected area and a stringent watch was kept for aliens. A 9.30 pm curfew was brought in for transport, and theatres and cinemas finished at 9.00 pm. Public houses were open to 10 pm but customers who remained until that hour had a long and often lonely walk home. Plymouth, before the war, had decided to scrap the trams but some tracks still remained, especially on the Peverell route, and available trams were brought back into use. British Restaurants were created to provide communal catering for those bombed out of their houses. One of the first was in the Girls' High School, North Hill; others were in the Guildhall, Hyde Park School and at Keyham and St Budeaux. All available space was used for growing food, so part of the Hoe was dug up and vegetables grown, and a Corporation piggery was created in an old farm in Central Park. Iron railings, gates etc from public and private buildings were removed to help the war effort. The police force was kept extremely busy but it was still regulation, well into 1943, for all policemen on duty to wear a respirator for half an hour every Tuesday afternoon. National League football was suspended and the gass grew high on the pitch. The Argyle stands were used as a furniture repository, only to be bombed in 1941. But local football survived with the formation of the Plymouth City Club and the Plymouth United Club with games against service teams. Greyhound racing was a major attraction at Plymouth Greyhound Stadium. Another example of life carrying on as normal was the continuous publication throughout the blitz of the *Western Evening Herald* and *Western Morning News*.

By the middle of 1943, of the 12,000 children who had been evacuated, 8,000 had returned, but 90 schools had been destroyed or seriously damaged and many secondary schools had moved to other towns. Devonport High School for Boys was evacuated to Penzance, Sutton Secondary School to St Austell and Devonport High for Girls to Tiverton. Plymouth Girls' School went to Newquay and St Boniface College to Buckfast Abbey, but Plymouth College stayed at Hyde Park Corner. Bombing raids continued through 1943 and 1944, the last on 30 April, but by then the City was able to cope more easily with each emergency. The 29th Division of the American Army arrived in 1943 and the American Navy established a base in the Cattewater. They brought with them many of their customs and activities. They introduced baseball and formed a team known as the Plymouth Yankees, playing on Saturday evenings at Pennycross Stadium. The gate receipts were given to local charities.

Preparations for the invasion of Europe were increasing and the US Army repeatedly practised landings on the long stretch of Slapton Sands for the 'great day'. The fleet was building up in the Sound and on 6 June 1944 the V and VII Corps of General Bradley's 1st Army embarked from Plymouth for the Normandy landings. Plymouth gradually relaxed. The blackout was dropped in September and the Home Guard stood down in November. The City was then able to count the cost of the blitz. 1,172 civilians had been killed and a further 3,276 injured. Casualties of service personnel must also have been great; 3,754 houses had been completely destroyed and a further 18,398 seriously damaged. Two Guildhalls, six hotels, eight cinemas, 26 schools, 41 churches and 100 public houses were among the buildings destroyed. The heart had been ripped out of the City, but already plans were well ahead for its reconstruction. The City was to rise again, fulfilling the chalked message 'Resurgam' which was nailed to St Andrew's Church after it had been bombed.

ABOVE: St Andrew's Church bombed. (LS) LEFT: Interior of St Andrew's
Church tidied up. (LS) RIGHT: Shopping disrupted. (LS)

LEFT: Damage to Royal Sailor's Rest, Devonport. (LS)RIGHT: Spooner's Corner, 21 March, 1941. (LS)
BELOW: Western National 'bus depot, Laira after a bombing raid. (LS)

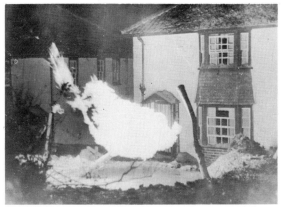

LEFT: Gas main explosion, Railway House, Peverell. (LS) RIGHT: Bewilderment at what was happening. (LS)
BELOW and OVERLEAF: City centre damage. (LS)

103

ABOVE: City centre damage. BELOW: Barrage balloon crew. (LS)

LEFT: Bomb disposal crew. (LS) RIGHT: Book stack in shell of bombed library. (LS) BELOW: Victory Parade, Tavistock Road, VE-Day. (LS)

ABOVE: Victory Parade, City centre. (LS) BELOW and OVERLEAF:
Street parties to celebrate victory. (LS)

107

A New Beginning

The extent of the bomb damage made it abundantly clear, even before the end of the blitz, that a massive reconstruction of the City centre would be needed. The task of producing a plan fell to James Paton Watson, the city engineer, and Professor Patrick Abercrombie of London University. Professor Abercrombie was involved at the invitation of Lord Astor and the Emergency Committee. After many drafts and alterations, *The Plan for Plymouth* was published in 1943 and approved in principle by the Council in August 1944. But there was much behind-the-scenes political activity; Lord Astor found himself in difficulty, unable to be chairman of the Reconstruction Committee, set up to implement the Paton Watson-Abercrombie Plan. In 1944, partly through ill-health, he did not seek re-election as Lord Mayor. Thus ended a period of unique dedication by one man to a city and its inhabitants.

The *Plan for Plymouth* was an extremely bold and enterprising scheme for the entire City. Plymouth, even before the Second World War, was in need of a complete overhaul, with more drastic changes required than could be initiated under existing planning powers. The significance of the shopping centre had grown out of all proportion to its narrow streets and cramped site. Traffic congestion was a serious problem. The Gothic style Civic Centre had become too small to house efficiently the staff needed to administer a large city. Slum clearance and rehousing schemes were barely keeping pace with needs and an unplanned sprawl was eroding the countryside. War damage provided the ideal opportunity to create something positive and practical rather than to patch and renovate. The Plan attempted to forecast a great modern city, a fit place for people to live and work in, safeguarding its links with the past and preparing for a prosperous future.

A number of activities, associated with the City, were identified in the Plan. The City functioned as a Naval Dockyard, Naval and Military Centre, a shopping centre for a wide area, a light industrial centre, a port for sea and air, a fishing port and a residential centre. This is reflected in the employment statistics of the time with 25% of insured persons associated with the Dockyard, 21% with distributive trades, 17% with building and public works and 4% in the hotel and boarding-house industry.

The National Uthwatt Committee had recommended that legislation should be introduced permitting a local authority to declare war damage and obsolete areas 'Reconstruction Areas' with power of acquisition at 1939 values. The Plymouth Plan recommended that the area south and west of the GWR line from Weston Mill Creek to North Road Station, bounded by North Road, Clifton Place, Greenbank and Tothill Roads and then to the River Plym should be so designated. Areas were to be set aside for industrial development in the Millbay-Stonehouse district between Union Street, West Hoe Road, Millbay Docks and the Royal Marine Barracks and also in the zone betwwen Sutton Harbour and Prince Rock. Marsh Mills was suggested as a site for light industry; an option taken up later by Tecalemit.

The whole city was divided into a series of Community and Neighbourhood Groups and Residential Units. Residential Units were based on a nursery school and Neighbourhood Groups, of 6-10,000 people, were based on an Elementary School. Five or six Neighbourhood

Groups would form a Community Group.

Comprehensive replanning was envisaged in Stonehouse, north of Union Street, where the residential area would be divided into two community units, based upon schools. The units were designed round neighbourhood centres with open space allocated on the basis of four acres per thousand of the population. The whole of the residential area was planned as a precinct in which no child would have to cross a main traffic route from home to school.

As it turned out, it is only the City centre part of the Plan that has really materialized. It had been anticipated that the Admiralty would take over a large part of Devonport and accordingly all shopping facilities were planned for the centre of Plymouth. The Admiralty at first wanted 220 acres, but was eventually satisfied with 50 acres divided between the Fore Street area and the zone outside the old Keyham Gates. The original plan for the centre of Plymouth envisaged a series of precinct units. There was to be a civic group based on St Andrew's Church, a rebuilt Guildhall and a shopping centre, largely based on its present position. A theatre group was planned in the Derry's Cross area, based on the Royal Cinema, with a new concert hall and theatre. Somewhat belatedly, the Theatre Royal has risen on this spot. Portland Square was to be the centre for an educational and cultural group. This has come to fruition with the Polytechnic and associated units. A series of enterprising schemes was suggested for a West Hoe recreation precinct. This was to be the marine entrance to Plymouth with a new centre for conference and amusements, an open-air theatre, a stadium and a great rotunda. The station at the Great Western Passenger Dock would bring visitors direct to this centre. The plan for the Barbican area was to rehabilitate the good buildings and to restore those of 'ancient lineage' whose features had been defaced over the years. It was even proposed to build a wall demarcating the old historic core from the centre. This was to run west from the Citadel at the top of Lambhay Hill, north on a line of the Hoe and St Andrew's and Kinterbury Street, passing the east end of St Andrew's Church. Then it was to run east to Charles Church and end near the site of Friary Gate at the north-east side of Sutton Harbour.

The ultimate design of the shopping centre is nearest to the original plan. It was argued that any attempt to relieve congestion by the mere widening of existing routes was doomed to failure. Each unit in the new shopping centre was designed so that through traffic was discouraged. The great N-S axis was planned as almost a 'triumphal way' linking a redesigned North Road Station with the top of the Hoe. This became Armada Way and is one of the more striking features of the City. Royal Parade became the major E-W axis with a dual carriageway and a 75 feet wide central reservation, laid out as a series of gardens.

It was stressed, at the outset, that the Plan would have to be sectionalized and carried out over a number of years. This is exactly what has happened and, in the process, a number of schemes have been modified and others dropped completely. The first kerbstone was laid on 17 March 1947, in Raleigh Lane, and on 29 October, King George VI performed the formal opening ceremony. The first new departmental store, Dingle's, was opened in 1951 and by 1955 most of Royal Parade and New George Street was completed. The Guildhall was rebuilt to the designs created by the City architect H. J. W. Stirling and was opened in 1959 by Field-Marshal Lord Montgomery. The Civic Centre was opened by HM the Queen in 1962 and the new Law Courts, by Lord Denning, in the following year. The shopping centre was virtually completed in 1971 by the rebuilding and pedestrianization of Drake's Circus. The City centre has received a number of criticisms over the years but there is no denying that it is one of the most comprehensive shopping centres in the country.

After the war, the people returned to the City they had been forced to leave and the population soon began to rise to its pre-war level. The reconstruction of the City centre was an urgent need but the provision of new housing for the homeless was a desperate necessity. It was estimated that nearly 20,000 houses would be required in the 10 years from 1945. This figure included 6,833 houses destroyed in the blitz, 6,277 slum or 'blighted' properties needing replacement and about 1,000 houses to take account of the pre-war shortage. The magnitude of the task can be appreciated when it is remembered that 11,159 houses were built in the 21 years between the wars.

Prefabricated buildings satisfied the short-term demand but new housing estates were needed to provide a lasting solution. Although many of the ideas for residential devlopment embodied in *The Plan for Plymouth* were never put into effect, some of the thinking behind those ideas was incorporated in new housing estates. The first of these was at Efford, followed by Ham, Honicknowle, Kings Tamerton, Ernesettle and Whitleigh. The estates were planned as comprehensive entities with shopping centres, schools and entertainment facilities. The target of 20,000 houses was passed in 1964, somewhat later than envisaged, but nevertheless, this represents an impressive scale of building. Some of these were private developments and over 800 houses were built by the Admiralty. This level of development could only be achieved by spreading into the surrounding countryside. After much hectic debate, Plymouth was able to extend its boundary in 1951 to include Tamerton and Roborough. But Plympton and Plymstock, fast developing areas, were still outside the Plymouth boundary and were not incorporated until 1967. More recently housing schemes have taken place at Leigham, Estover, Bellever and Chaddlewood.

The diversification of the industrial base of the City was another priority. There were repeated fears that the Naval presence at Devonport would diminish and that employment in the Dockyard would be drastically cut. Only six new ships were laid down in the post-war period, the last of these, the Leander Class frigate HMS *Scylla*, launched in 1968. The association of Devonport with the large aircraft carriers also came to an end when HMS *Ark Royal* was paid off in December 1978. But the Dockyard escaped the drastic cuts that other Naval dockyards faced in 1981, and a number of developments have maintained it as a major Naval base. In 1977 Dr David Owen, MP for Devonport and the then Foreign Secretary, opened a new frigate complex in which three frigates can be dry docked completely under cover. Then in 1978 the then Prime Minister, James Callaghan opened a new Fleet Maintenance Base, and in 1980, HRH the Prince of Wales opened the new submarine Refit Complex.

Even though the Dockyard appears to have a safe future, it is unwise to rely too heavily on it for future employment. Thus the City has made a great effort to attract new industry. The first new firms had arrived immediately after the war. These were Tecalemit at Marsh Mills, Berketex at Honicknowle and Rank at Ernsettle. New land was set aside at Burrington, Estover and Southway and many national and international companies were persuaded to set up factories. This was aided initially in 1958 when Plymouth was designated a Development Area. This was rescinded in 1960 but it was partially restored as an Intermediate Development Area in 1969. More recent developments have taken place at Bellever and subsequently at Newnham, when Plympton became part of Plymouth. The employment base of the City is now more diversified than it has ever been.

The commercial ports have also seen major changes since 1945. It was inevitable that the increase in air transport would make the luxury liners of the inter-war years obsolete, but for a number of years, liner traffic was maintained. In the early 1950s over 20,000 passengers a year passed through Millbay but, by 1963, the trade was finished. A more recent upsurge has been provided by the Brittany Ferries service to St Malo and Roscoff, France, carrying over 200,000 passengers a year. An additional service to Santander, in northern Spain, was added in 1978. The ships are of the roll-on roll-off type and a new jetty was provided at Millbay Docks to accommodate lorry traffic attracted by the service . The number of ships using Sutton Harbour and the Cattewater declined steadily in the 1970s, coal at Sutton and petrol in, and china clay out of Cattedown being the only major commodities handled.

Fishing revived immediately after the war but declined again rapidly. An upsurge occurred in the 1970s, partly due to an extension of territorial waters and partly due to modern fishing methods. A new fish quay was added in 1967.

As commercial shipping declined, boating for pleasure increased. Occasions such as the Single-handed Transatlantic Races, the Fastnet and various round-the-world events, organised by the Royal Western Yacht Club, brought many yachts to the inner basin at Millbay. Less ambitious yachtsmen have been catered for in the new marinas at Sutton Harbour and at Ocean Quay, the latter backed by luxury flats. These developments will ensure that Plymouth remains firmly in the sea-faring tradition.

The post-war period was a stormy one for both local and national politics. All three Plymouth parliamentary seats were won by Labour candidates in the 1945 General Election. Michael Foot defeated Hore-Belisha, to take Devonport before being defeated by Joan Vickers. The number of constituencies was reduced to two in 1950 and Nancy Astor's son, J. J. Astor, held the Sutton seat from 1951-9. Joan Vickers, who had represented Devonport for almost twenty years, was eventually unseated by Dr David Owen.

On the local scene, a number of capable leaders, such as Harry Mason, Harry Wright and Harold Pattinson, came and went. The leadership of the Council also fluctuated between Labour and Conservative, but there were few major conflicts. The greatest change was brought about by the 1974 reorganisation of local government, when the county boroughs were reduced to district councils, with many of their responsibilities switching to the county councils. For the first time since Plymouth received its Act of Incorporation in 1439, it was ruled from outside. Although a number of prominent local politicians, such as George Creber, who, as well as being Conservative leader on the Plymouth Council, was also leader of Devon County Council, have battled hard for Plymouth, many are unhappy with the arrangement.

The period after the Second World War has seen the emergence of a new civic pride. From the ashes of the old, a new City has grown. Communications with the rest of the country are excellent; one of the last links, the Tamar Road Bridge, was opened by the Queen Mother in 1961. The Polytechnic has built up a national reputation for academic standards and additional educational possibilities have been provided by the College of St Mark and St John at Derriford. The new General Hospital, also at Derriford, provides the most up-to-date medical facilities. Civic pride is also reflected in the Theatre Royal, opened in 1982, and the appearance of local conservation societies, whose aim is to preserve the best of the City's past. The work of these societies, such as the Stonehouse and Barbican Associations, was prominent in the displays and publications during European Architectural Heritage year in 1975. The past has been kept alive vividly by Mayflower Year 1972, the 350th anniversary of the sailing of the Pilgrim Fathers. It is to be hoped that the future of the City which 'bears the noble name' of Plymouth, will be as illustrious as its past.

ABOVE: War memorial on the Hoe. LEFT: Smeaton's Tower on the Hoe. (LS) RIGHT: Anchor from HMS *Ark Royal* In Armada Way.

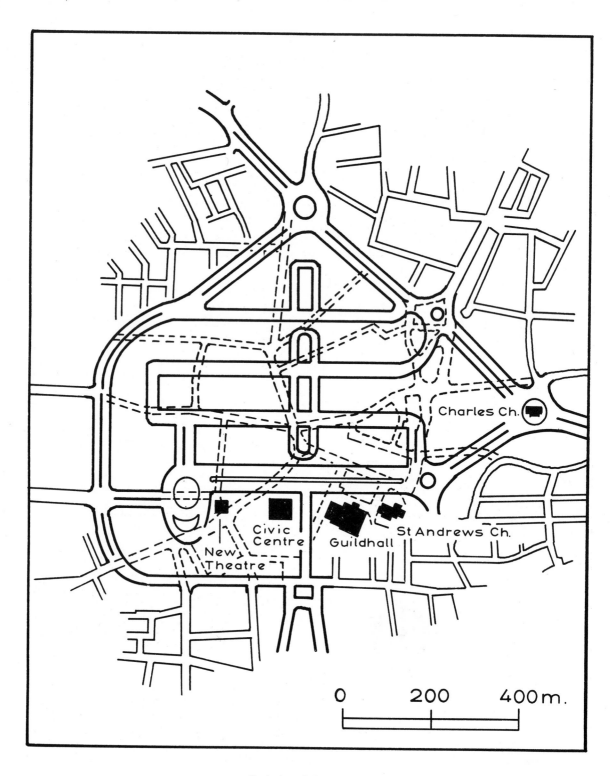

Redesigned city centre.

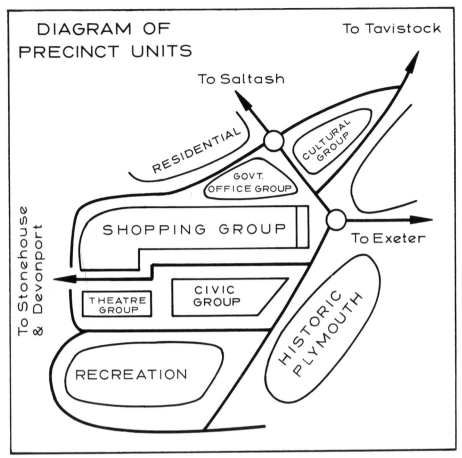

DIAGRAM OF PRECINCT UNITS

To Tavistock

To Saltash

RESIDENTIAL

CULTURAL GROUP

GOVT. OFFICE GROUP

SHOPPING GROUP

To Exeter

To Stonehouse & Devonport

THEATRE GROUP

CIVIC GROUP

HISTORIC PLYMOUTH

RECREATION

ABOVE: Proposed precinct units in the new City centre. BELOW: New Civic Centre.

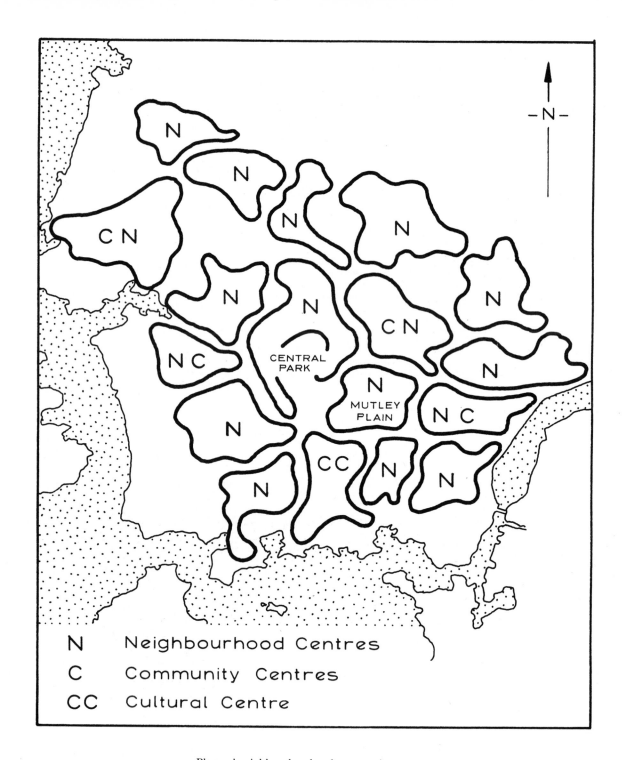

N   Neighbourhood Centres
C   Community Centres
CC   Cultural Centre

Planned neighbourhood and community centres.

LEFT: New Civic Centre. BELOW: Frankfort Gate and New Market. (LS) RIGHT: View west from the Civic Centre. (LS)

ABOVE: View from Devonport. (LS) BELOW: Victoria Wharves, Cattedown. (LS)

LEFT: Tamar Road Bridge under construction. (LS) RIGHT: Bristol double decker on the Torquay route. (LS)
BELOW: Festival of Britain tapestry, 1951. (LS)

LEFT: *Mayflower II*. (LS) RIGHT: The 'old' and 'new' combined. (GD) BELOW: The modern Plymouth Station. (GD)

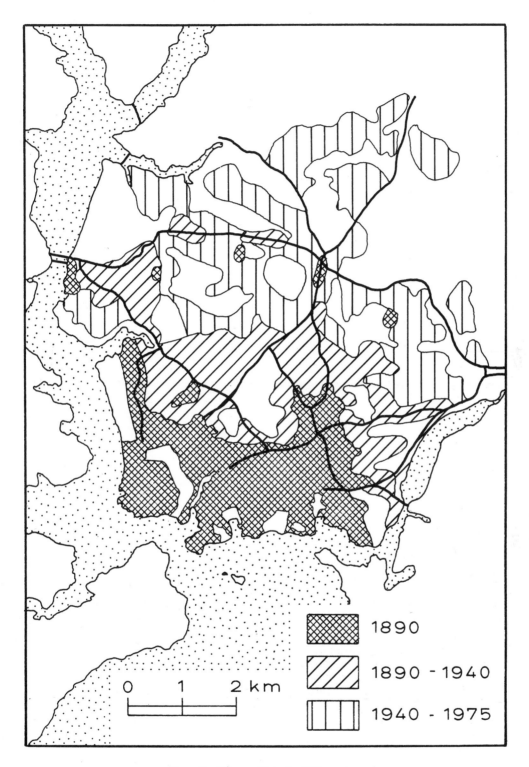

Growth of Plymouth in the 20th century.

ABOVE: Mutton Cove, once a stopping place for the Cremyll Ferry. (LS)
LEFT: Brittany ferry *Armorique*, operating the Plymouth-Roscoff service.
(WMN) RIGHT: Sir Francis Chichester and *Gypsy Moth IV*, in which he
sailed single-handed around the world. (WMN)

ABOVE: Barbican Fish Quay, 1982. BELOW: New marina, Sutton Harbour.

Bibliography

Any author owes much to previously published work. The literature on Plymouth is quite substantial but the books by R.N. Worth (1890), C.W. Bracken (1931) and Crispen Gill (1966, 1979) are worth a special mention. The list below is not exhaustive but indicates the range of published work available. More detailed accounts of specific aspects are plentiful in the Transactions of the Plymouth Institution and the Devonshire Association. In addition, 19th century guides, directories and newspapers provide a flavour of the City at that time, while the Local History Section of Plymouth Central Library possesses a number of unpublished manuscripts.

Barnicott, R. *Plymouth in History*. Cornubian Press, London 1906.

Bracken, C.W. *History of Plymouth*, Plymouth 1931 (reprinted 1970, Wakefield).

Burns, K.V. *Devonport Built Warships since 1860*, Liskeard 1981.

Burt, W. *Review of the Mercantile State of Plymouth*, Plymouth 1815.

Burt, W. *Review of the Port of Plymouth*, Plymouth 1816.

Dicker, G. *A Short History of Devonport Dockyard*, Plymouth 1969.

Gaskell-Brown, C (ed) *Industrial Archaelogy of Plymouth*, Plymouth 1973.

Gill, Crispin. *Plymouth, A New History. Ice Age to the Elizabethans*. David and Charles, 1966.

Gill, Crispin. *Plymouth in Pictures*, David and Charles, 1968.

Gill, Crispin. *Sutton Harbour*, Plymouth, 1970.

Gill, Crispin. *Plymouth, A New History. 1603 to the Present Day*. David and Charles, 1979.

Hamilton-Edwards, Gerald. *Twelve Men of Plymouth*, Plymouth 1951.

Jewitt, L. *History of Plymouth*, Plymouth 1873.

Majdalany, F. *The Red Rocks of Eddystone*, Longmans 1959 (paperback 1962).

Rowe, R.B. *Ecclesiastical History of Plymouth*, Plymouth 1876.

Salmon A.L. *The Story of English Towns: Plymouth*, London 1920.

Sambourne, R.C. *Plymouth, 100 Years of Street Travel*, Glasney, 1974.

Savignon, A. *With Plymouth Through Fire*, Hayle 1968.

Stephens, W. *Highways and Byways of Plymouth*, Plymouth 1943.

Trewin, J.C. *Portrait of Plymouth*, Hale 1973.

Twyford, H.P. *It Came to Our Door*, Plymouth 1945.

Walling, R.A.J. *The Story of Plymouth*, Westaway Books, 1950.

Watson, J. Paton and Abercombie, P. *A Plan for Plymouth*, Plymouth 1943.

Whitfield, H.F. *Plymouth and Devonport in times of War and Peace*, Plymouth 1900.

Wintle, F. *The Plymouth Blitz*, Bodmin 1981.

Worth, R.N. *History of the Town and Borough of Devonport*, Plymouth 1870.

Worth, R.N. *History of Plymouth*, Brendon and Son, 1890.

Worth, R.N. *Calendar of Plymouth Municipal Records*, Plymouth 1893.

Wright, W.H.K. *Illustrated Commercial Guide to Plymouth and District*, Plymouth 1894.

Model of the new Theatre Royal, Derry's Cross. (WMN)

127

LEFT: Mackerel fleet in Millbay Docks, January 1980. (WMN) RIGHT: Start of the trawler race: part of the annual Sutton Harbour Regatta. (WMN)

ENDPAPERS: FRONT — Devonport and Stonehouse in 1821.
BACK — Plymouth City centre before the blitz.

Subscribers

Presentation Copies

1. **Plymouth City Corporation**
2. **Devon County Council**
3. **Plymouth City Library**
4. **Devon County Library**
5. **Plymouth City Museum and Art Gallery**
6. **Councillor R.C.J. Scott**

7. John & Judith Gerrard
8. Clive & Carolyn Birch
9. A. Yarde
10. Mrs M. Hard
11. Mr Bromage
12. C.H. Robertson
13. Mrs Janet Gearon
14. Mrs Allan
15. R. Organ
16. G.A. Atkinson
17. Mrs D. Burgess
18. Mrs M. O'Hagan
19. M. Sutcliffe
20. P. Blake
21. Mr & Mrs B. Boulden
22. Mr & Mrs J.C. Finch
23. Mr & Mrs J. Todd
24. Mrs Jennings
25. John Luscombe
26. M.A. Johnson
27. R. Fraser
28. K. Coaker
29. Mrs C. Douglas
30. M.J. Lynden
31. B.J. Ritson
32. P.D. Billing
33. G.D. Farr
34. Mrs A. Farr
35. K.R. Hill
36. Peter Chard
37. Miss A.E. Upcott
38. Malcolm Read
39. Victoria & Albert Museum
40. B.S. Kiek
41. Mrs E.V. Martyn
42. B.A. Foote
43. M. Norman
44. A. Martin
45. Mrs J. Breed
46. K. Bates
47. F. Sage
48. Mr & Mrs J.C. Sutton
59. Jean Richards
50. E. Ham
51. B.E. Dolbear
52. Mrs Sheila Rogerson
53. R. Waterfield
54. K.H. Taylor
55. Mrs S.J. Smith
56. P.S. Phillips
57. S.P. Wood
58. F.V.J. Coniam
59. Mrs C.J. Austin
60. F.A. Kenny
61. S.J. Mayer
62. A.C.G. Tomlinson
63. W.N. Thorning
64. / 65. Mrs A.M. Bunker
66. J.S. Falzon
67. C.H. Williams
68. J.T. Sings
69. Mrs M. Mumford

70. C.S. Mumford
71. John Deacon
72. Mrs Vera Deacon
73. F.R. Neville
74. Mr & Mrs P.A. Turpin
75. B.K. Gorvin
76. J. Adams
77. Mrs J.E. Heath
78. Mrs D.M. Rothery
79. Mrs D. Nichols
80. Mrs L.M. Andrew
81. Mrs R.F. Knott
82. J.A. Doyle
83. Mrs R. Demellweek
84. Mrs A. Whitman
85. Mrs J. Yule
86. Mrs M.E. Floyd
87. Mrs G.W. Distin
88. Mrs J. Taskis
89. D.F. Northcott
90. A.J. Landricombe
91. Ms Jennie James
92. Mrs R.M. Webber
93. Mrs E.A. Bennett
94. F.J. Pengilly
95. Peter Pearce
96. Stanley Cox
97. Robert J. Rickard
98. C. James Vassie
99. Mrs E. Borovkoff
100. T.C. Hodge
101. J. Stafford
102. L. Smith
103. R.A. Boyes
104. Dr R.A. Cardwell
105. N. Stafford
106. Mrs D.M. Trethowa
107. Mrs G.M. Launce
108. H. Burer
109. C. Smith
110. G.J. Boyes
111. C.F. Thuell
112. T. Drean
113. Mr & Mrs P.H. Andrew
114. Miss E.A. Williams
115. Miss C.B.E. Hales
116. Mrs T.M. Elliott
117. S.L. Crocker
118. R. Willing
119. E.F. Page

120. J. Guest
121. Mrs B. Everrett
122. B. Couch
123. R.S. Smart
124. W.F. Webber
125. Mrs J.C. Sanders
126. Mrs A. Simpson
127. W.J. Coles
128. C.J.H. Hocking
129. Miss S. Willis
130. D.A. Cann
131. R.B. Moore
132. Dr S.I. Egglestone
133. John & Susan Bateman
134. Mrs C.E. Wharton
135. T.C. Quest
136. J.W. Mitchelmore
137. Anthony J. Gillhespy
138. Ian M. Gillhespy
139. Mrs N.S. Roxburgh
140. M.J. Campin
141. Miss B.L. Rutter
142. Plymouth Polytechnic Library
143. John L. Knight
144. F.E. Sandercock
145. Major A.J. Biscombe MBE
146. R.J. Feneck
147. Cllr & Mrs A. Rushby
148. A. Freeman
149. J. Blake
150. Miss S.B. Burch
151. Mrs M. Baker
152. E.W. Webb
153. W.F. Foster
154. Mrs K. Sheridan
155. Mrs J. Dixon
156. Miss B. Langham
157. D.F. Leach
158. Mr & Mrs M.D. Gilruth
159. J.J. Penfound
160. Mrs C.A. Temme
161. F. Chambers
162. J.B. Andrews
163. Mrs J.M. Hardwell
164. L.J. Johnson
165. S.E. Forrow
166. K. Willcocks
167. R.V. Stear

168. M.K.J. Trend
169. R.G. Spettigue
170. T.F. Jones
171. / 172. Mr & Mrs F. Bryant
173. P.J. Smith
174. Mrs S. Brown
175. Mrs A.E. Dawson
176. Mrs S. Potter
177. Mrs P.H. Smith
178. Mrs J.B. Rundle
179. Mrs J. Henderson
180. Mr & Mrs B. Lintell
181. B.B. Lugg
182. A.J. Clarke
183. L.A. Griffiths
184. Mrs J. Tothill
185. V.J. Payne
186. A.F. Moore
187. W.W. Coram
188. E.A. Sparkes
189. C.H. Smith
190. P.A. Love
191. Mr P.F. & Mrs V.P. Sampson
192. R.J. Dunlop
193. / 194. Mrs J. Tothill
195. Mr & Mrs M.V. Finn
196. Andrew Cooper
197. Ingrid Cooper
198. George Cooper
199. Mrs J.A. Hartnell
200. / 201. Mrs M. Fragell
202. Kerrie Elizabeth Sutton
203. M.F. Parry
204. K. Aspinall
205. J. Bodenham
206. W.J. Warren
207. G. Banning
208. Mrs Dean
209. Mr Dean
210. Mr & Mrs M.V. Finn
211. / 212. W.J. Warren
213. Mrs A.M. Perkins
214. A.C. Ratcliffe
215. Mrs T. Symons
216. Mr & Mrs J.R. Munn
217. Mrs T. Symons
218. G. Waterfield
219. Mrs P.W. Podmore
220. C.E. Davies
221. K.C. Ridge
222. Mrs M.J. Peathey Johns
223. D.J. Bolgar
224. Mrs Irene James
225. Mrs J. Deveney
226. R. Smith
227. B. Lavery
228. Mrs J. Joyner
229. Mrs B. Atwill

230 Mrs M.B. Pope
231 W.J. Croston
232 Mrs J. Ford
233 J. Harris
234 Mrs N. Lee
235 R.S. Algar
236 L.G. Jane
237 M.C.F. Ware
238 Mrs D. Phillips
239 Mr & Mrs E. Rutton
240 B.J. Ellis
241 K. Potter
242 Mrs E. Raywood
243 Miss L.A. Neville
244 H. Hicks
245 J.M. Mann
246 D.J. Smith
247 Mrs S.A. Sullivan
248 Mrs M. Bell
249 Mr & Mrs B.W. Cooper
250 A.G. Smith
251 P.A. Sutcliffe
252 N. Reed
253 P. Andrews
254 D.J. Howkins
255 S.H. Thorn
256 Mrs Augusta C. Train
257 Mrs A.M.L. Gould
258 Mrs J. White
259 Mrs G. Nick Sinclair
260 Miss E.M. Eason
261 P.H. Jutson
262 R.W. Bolt
263 Mrs I.L. Harkin
264 E.J. Ryder
265 D.H. & J.P. Griffiths
266 Mrs J. MacManus
267 Mrs Hatch
268 L. Buckton
269 R.L. Collins
270 Mrs K. Stacey
271 Ms I. Van Goch & Mr R. Fraser
272 Mrs B. Loveless
273 Mrs M. Barrett
274 Mrs A. Tills
275 Mrs P. Thorne
276 T.H.C. Richards
277 D.A. Evans
278 279 Mrs Heath
280 J.T. Veale
281 Gary Collings
282 M.S. Whitting
283 P.A. Hancock
284 Mr & Mrs D.A. Turpin
285 Mr & Mrs A. Cock
286 Mrs Hilary Cobbett
287 Mrs Glenys Hitzig and Family
288 C.J.F. Pollard
289 W. Dart
290 Mrs P. Hughes

291 Rev W. Babcock Fitch
292 Rev Peter J. Gregson
293 A. John
294 K. Lewis
295 Mrs Jennifer Macpherson
296 Mrs C.S. Earl
297 Mrs J.C. Pick
298 L. Hooper
299 Mrs J. Straw
300 M.A. Sewell
301 C.A. Snell
302 John Jones
303 N.C. Griffin
304 Mrs M.L. Honey
305 M.J. Hocking
306 P.R. Stabb
307 Mrs J.E. Barkham
308 N.G. Hocking
309 J. Hey
310 Mrs J.F. Law
311 W.F.E. Eustace-Pedlar
312 R. Trewhella
313 R.J. Whitfield
314 Mrs M.J. Gregg
315 K.A. Frood
316 M. Prout
317 Mrs J. Warne
318 L.E. Aldridge
319 H.D. Sweeney
320 R.H.M Medway
321 Mrs G. Brimacombe
322 Richard Coe
323 Roger Aitken
324 A. Cross
325 W. Pascoe
326 H.J. Gates
327 R. Haskell
328 D. Arrowsmith
329 M.A. Welsford
330 T.E. Day
331 Mrs M. Hoodless
332 Finbar E. Nolan
333 W.G. Parker
334 R. Palfrey
335 Mrs Mahoney
336 Anthony J. Normington
337 Mrs E. Brown
338 S.J. Martin
339 Mrs D.M. Cook
340 M.C. Brown
341 A.G. Turner
342 S.S. Tanner
343 344 G. Bellamy
345 E. Johns
346 P.G. Parsons
347 H.T. Brown
348 S.A. Cooper
349 D.A. Corcoran
350 Keith Clayton Smith
351 Mrs B. Ricketts
352 G.H. Chudley

353 Leonard Walshaw
354 B.A. Quintrell
355 R.C. Dingle
356 E.M. Kiltie
357 A. Beahan
358 F.E. Barnes
359 L.C. McCoy
360 Miss P. Gilmore
361 Mrs Gilmore
362 Mrs J.M. Bryan
363 Mrs H.M. Rowe
364 R.F. Darton
365 Mrs J. Grant
366 A.J.B. Stevenson
367 Mr & Mrs J.L. McGregor
368 B.A. Roe
369 G. Hadfield
370 D. Wigmore
371 Mrs D.F. Sharp
372 David Moore
373 E.R. Luscombe
374 K.J. Buckingham
375 W. Ellis
376 A.J. Caffidy
377 L. McDermott-Brown
378 Cecil Eric Jones
379 C.R. Burrows
380 Mr & Mrs P.E. Barnes
381 Anthony Paul Cox
382 S.R.F. Morey
383 H. Pratt
384 Mrs D. Burley
385 Mrs V.A. Hay
386 Jack Cock
387 W.E. Foxsmith
388 Mrs A. Hamley
389 J.R. Owen
390 R.W. Cooper
391 K. Moate
392 F.A. Boulton
393 J.B. Wilkie
394 M. Helen Wilkie
395 Mrs Beryl Blackledg
396 Derek Keith Allen
397 J.S. Jacks
398 D.G. Hall
399 M.C.P. Newberry
400 M. Lilly
401 Mrs Blatchford
402 R.H. Baker
403 J. Manning
404 S.N. & J.D. Garbutt
405 A.M. & A. Blackbur
406 Mrs A.B. Hanks
407 J. McCall
408 P.J. Hanks
409 Mrs P.F. Cockram-Ashley
410 D. MacDonald
411 Mrs P. Raven
412 S.F. Fane
413 M.F. Fane
414 Mrs B.V. McCreadie
415 Mrs K. Brooks

416 G. Wright
417 D. Hill
418 Miss A. Hunt
419 Plymouth Atheneum
420 Mrs D. James
421 A. Barlow
422 Mrs J.F. Humphries
423 S. Robertson
424 Mrs S.E. Higgins
425 Ian Neville Jarvis
426 Jacques Chevrolle
427 Anne Chevrolle
428 J.R Cooper
429 C.G. Ellis
430 W.C. Connett
431 Miss V.C.M. Earl
432 G.J.R. Peace
433 W.C. Symons
434 J.M. Mears
435 John Malcolm Hoblyn
436 Mrs C. Page
437 Mrs S. Murphy
438 P.C. Hatton
439 J.C. Stabb
440 Patrick Whatty
441 G.W. Crotty
442 N.R. Buckingham
443 Mr & Mrs N.F. Schofield
444 L.J. Cann
445 Mrs B. Smelser
446 I. Mitchell
447 Mrs P. Mitchell
448 Mrs Sue M. Passmore
449 R.E.A. Smith
450 Mr & Mrs S. Talbott
451 R.E. Bunce
452 Mrs J. Woodward
453 Mrs Maureen Selley
454 Mrs B. Glynne
455 J. Bishop
456 Miss J.E. O'Brien
457 Mr & Mrs G. Sothcott
458 Mrs Diana Prideaux
459 Miss B. Jones
460 Miss J.E. Pearce
461 Charles Allinson
462 J. Day
463 R.B. Downing-Waite
464 Mrs N.M. Cobb
465 Mrs Monica Voden
466 Mr & Mrs L. Day
467 Mrs P. Leonard
468 Mrs Dianne Ball
469 R.E. Vickery
470 Mrs K. Geoffrey
471 Mr & Mrs M. Wallhead
472 Mrs J.E. Greenfield
473 A.E. Mardon
474 J.R.W. Harvey
475 Mrs J.M. Francis
476 Mrs Roberts
477 478 H. Duffield

479 K.G. Pooley	543 R. West	606 Mrs M.M. Bolt	670 Miss E.A. Roper
480 Mrs A. Toms	544 Mrs B.A. Hesp	607 R.J. Martin	671 E. Grigg
481 L. Hodge	545 Mr & Mrs John A.	608 Mrs D. Bennett	672 Mrs Ousey
482 Mrs B. Swiss	Curror	609 M.J. Killick	673 R.C. Scott
483 F.C. Pearce	546 F. Powell	610 F.J. Campbell	674 E.H. Smith
484 D.J. Riddle	547 Mrs M. Witts	611 H. Pritchard	675 Nigel Hannaford
485 Mrs M. Flaherty	548 R.E. Vineer	613	676 Mrs Bailey
486 Mrs Trick	549 Mark F. Kerr	614 Mrs Hodkinson	677 Mrs Keast
487 Mrs M.I. Walls	550 Mrs S. Dawes	615 Mrs M. Coniam	678 Rev Wyatt
488 D.W. Fisher	551 F.J. Brooks	616 Dr M.P. Stratford	679 Southway Junior
489 J.A. Fisher	552 I. Creamer	617 N.C. Coles	School
490 A.C.J. Fisher	553 K.M. May	618 Mr & Mrs J. Pedley	680 Mrs P.L. Irving
491 Mrs S.K. Derslev	554 F.D. Vowles	619 A.F.P. Wheeler	681 Mrs J.M. Weddle
492 Norman Edward Parker	555 G.A. Burley	620 A.S. Jones	682 Mrs F.L. Yearling
493 Mrs B.E.S. Thompson	556 R.S. Soper	621 V.H. Deacon	683 O. Curry
494 J.C. Carpenter	557 R.W. Floyd	622 Mrs P. Porter	684 H.A. Bate
495 G. Brooks	558 Mrs I.E. Burrows	623 P.S. Briggs	685 L. Hooper
496 D. Milne	559 T.J.R. Lovett	624 Mrs Marilyn T. Ferris	686 Mrs B. Macfarlane
497 P.A. Beeney	560 Mrs S. Pickford	625 Mrs M. Hipwell	687 K. Sambrook
498 S. Taskis	561 Mrs T. Carpenter	626 Mrs Janet Brown	688 Mrs K. George
499 J.F. Cotter	562 Dr & Mrs M.H. Owen	627 W.P. Gilbert	689 Jack Jenkin
500 D.J. McFeat	563 Mrs R. Shepherd	628 J.S. Smale	690 Colin W. Stephens
501 Mrs J.M. Glasson	564 M.R. Spry	629 A.B. Gore	691 R.E, Brown
502 Mrs K. Bond	565 Mrs J. Warren	630 Mrs J. MacPherson	692 P. Stancombe
503 Nathan Paul Groves	566 J.H. Rundle	631 Mrs W.J. Picken	693 Miss B. Bryant
504 Mrs D. Tozer	567 Mrs E.L. Sage	632 D. Jeffery	694 B.P. Collins
505 Mrs B.P. Tomlinson	568 Roma L. Baker	633 Mr Mark	695 Mrs Sue Duke
506 Miss E.G. Yelland	569 P.J. Sharpe	634 Mrs J. Bayly	696 Mrs A. Edgecombe
507 Mrs L. Boethwick	570 Alan A. Hargreaves	635 R. O'Leary	697 Colin Alexander
508 S.T. Martin	571	636 Mr Ley	Smith
509 Mrs P. Bartrop	572 W.G. Tozer	637 Mrs Ley	698 Mrs J.M. Wherry
510 Mrs L. Pearce	573 P. Sheldon	638 Mr Wortelhock	699 Miss N.M. Batstone
511 G.E. Barnes	574 A.S. Cortis	639 Miss J. Cobbledick	700 F.R. Collings
512 D. Green	575 Mrs E. Mankey	640 Mr Fitzpatrick	701 Mrs P. Membrey
513 D.E. Beadell	576 Mrs E. Tucker	641 W.J. Picken	702 C. Passmore
514 E.A. Simms	577 Mrs V.J. Reed	642 Anthony N. Lake	703 Mrs L.A. Wells
515 B.E. Simms	578 G. Eden	643 A.A. Hawkins	704 C. Nile
516 R. Fifield	579 A.D. Chamberlain	644 Mrs M.S. Seward	705 G.R. Hill
517 Mrs J. Knapman	580 Michael Frost	645 Mrs F. Rundle	706 N. Cummins
518 R.C. Deane	581 Stuart Lloyd	646 E.J. Sutton	707 B.J. Edwards
519 Alan W. Derry	582 Sarah Andrews	647 D.F. Budge	708 R.H. Sterry
520 Anthony K. Robb	583 A.G. Chick	648 W. Henry	709 D.B. Hill
521 A. Yalden	584 A. Yabsley	649 C.M. Rendle	710 Mrs E. Partridge
522 R.K. Palfrey	585 Mr & Mrs R. Simpson	650 Miss M. Smith	711 F.C. Crook
523 A.J.A. Hollett	586 E. Wood	651 Capt. Lumley-	712 R.F. Eglimtom
524 J. Fisher	587 G.W. Woodfine	Harvatt	713 Miss E. Lake
525 Brian Leslie Cork	588 Mr & Mrs F. Cadby	652 Capt A.M.W.	714 R.O. Lenkiewicz
526 E.J. Jewitt	589 Mrs M.J. Greaves	Goddard	715 E.W. Luscombe
527 David J.W. Hay	590 Mrs Stephens	653 Mrs Sheering	716 H. Simpson
528 C.L. Bennett	591 Mrs M. Cook	654 Mr Hamlyn	717 S. Horn
529 B. Rolls	592 L.J.W. Casey	655 Mrs J. Yates	718 Cllr George Creber
530 D. Russah	593 Mrs Lee	656 Mrs E. Gray	719 V.J. Wallen
531 J.R. Rea	594 H. Hajee	657 N.H. Sparks	720 Jane Edward
532 G. Ladner	595 Mrs Middleton	658 K.G.R. Hazelden	721 Norman Sitters
533 Mrs D. Burch	596 R. Harris	659 Mrs T.M. Elliott	722 Ronald G. Smith
534 Mr & Mrs Weatherly	597 Miss Hill	660 Mrs G.M.E. Lawton	723 Mr & Mrs B.F. Blades
535 J.P. Ferris	598 Mr Page	661 Mr Blee	724
536 R.M. Pickles	599 Mr Sampson	662 A.H. Warren	725 C.J. Pidduck
537 L.S. Bunker	600 J.A. Bishop	663 R. Blanchard	726 R.S. Taylor CER
538 Mrs N. Taylor	601 Mr Crispin	664 T. Hugo	727 Mr Seymour-Jones
539 J. Scott	602 W.T. Ainsworth	665 B. Prince	728 T.E. Hardy
540 Mr & Mrs David G.	603 W. Sibley	666 Miss B. Pearson	729 Mrs C. Knights
Spear	604 Mr & Mrs A.L. Clarke	667 F.G. Edwards	730 B. Buckingham
541 Mrs Anne France	605 Mr & Mrs B.J.	668 Mrs C.E. Roper	731 Mrs Hoskin
542 K.H. Woodward	Blatchford	669 D.J. Roper	732 S.W. Seldon

131

733 R.W. Marks	797 Mrs Diana Lawer	860 Bruce Burley	942 E.J. Giles
734 B.E. Ritchie	798 L. Gerrard	861 T.A. O'Connor	943 Mr & Mrs P.W.G.
735 C.T. Brophy	799 Mrs P. Woodhouse	862 David E. Lewis	Coombs
736 Mrs L.B. Waits	800 Mr & Mrs G. Jennings	863 W.L. McBride	944 P. Maunder
737 D.G. Reed	801 A.E. Henly	864 T.C. Hawken	945 A.J. Blagden
738 Richard Paynter	802 A.H. Doughty	865 D. Scoble	946 Michael Rice
739 Mrs P.E. Phelps	803 Mrs J.M. Boase	866 Mrs E.A. Tarr	947
740 Miss M. Murphy	804 Mrs I.L. Fulfit	867 Cornwall County	Mrs D. Johnson
741 D. Lock	805 Mr & Mrs A.W.	Library	948
742 Mrs S. Guyler	Sommer	885 Hillside School	949 Mrs W. Bridgeman
743 E.L. Adams	806 L.A. Veale	886	950 Mrs Goddard
744 Mrs J.E.M. Bristow	807 Mrs W.I. Veale	887 H. Davies	951 D.J. Westlake
745 Peter Holloway	808 W.J.J. Dovall	888 Laira Green Primary	952 E.W. Torr
746 D. Urry	809 G.B. Doidge	School	953 D.M. Muirhead
747 R.M.D. Trevan	810 R.D. Milford	889 G.R. Sloggett	954 Tamerton Vale
748 B.S. Libby	811 Mrs W.M. Elliot	890	County Primary
749 P. Lidstone	812 David Harvey	R. Harrop	School
750 E. Hooper	813 R.G. Tozer	895	955 G. Bloom
751 Jeremy Swift	814 R. Edgcumbe	896 S.R. Coverley BM	956 Mrs N.J. Hamilton
752 S.J.F. Roberts	815 J.W.L. Edgcumbe	897 Guy Fleming	957
753 Miss C.C. Roberts	816 Guy Fleming	898 Elaine S.S. Malins	T.J. Mole
754 Miss A. Cutter	817 Mrs C.V. Williams	899 Capt R. Lumley-	958
755 Mrs C.T. Fox	818 J.E.R. Henly	Harvatt (Royal	959 Kenneth J. Treeby
756 Mrs Huttel	819 Miss G. Digby	Marines)	960 L.D. Totterdell
757 P.C. Holt	820 R. Elliott	900 D.B. Jeffrey	961 C.H. Vickery
758 B. Docwra	821 A.F. Sargent	901 H. Whatley & Co Ltd	962 J.F. James
759 Mrs Eileen M. Arnold	822 N.S. Mitchell	902 Crouse-Hinds UK Ltd	963 K.M. Higginson
760 C.T. Brophy	823 Miss I. Savage	903 Miss May Garland	964 D.J. Cliffe
761 D.G. Harris	824 F.J. Pring	904	965 Dorothy Redhead
762 D.J. Hick	825 Mrs K. Pritchard	Crouse-Hinds UK Ltd	966 Roger Phillips
763 R.B. Hick	826 C.C. Taylor	908	967 Mrs L.E. Jones
764 L.R. May	827 K.M.G. Huxham	909 Anthony G.A. Wates	968 J.J. Jones
765 S. Mitchell	828 D.R. Lem-Mon	910 A.H. Grant	969 J.A. Dunnan
766 B.A. Norman	829 Mrs P.R. Spokes	911 Mrs A.N. Larkworthy	970 K.A. Bell
767	830 G. Towers	912	971
J. Barber	831 Eric David Wyatt	L.J. Turpin	E.P. Cross
768	832 Richard Weaver	913	972
769 Mrs E. Boon	833 Mark Weaver	914 D.J. Hawkings	973 Miss L.J. Hargreaves
770 G. Baker	834 Mrs Jacquie	915 David Rice	974 Richard John
771 D.F. Stead	MacGillivray	916 J.C. Campbell	Collings
772 F. Lucas	835 A.R. Banbury	917 Foot & Bowden	975 C.C. Turner
773 Miss D Jonas	836 Mrs Harding	918 D.J. Fraser	976 Mrs Margaret M.
774 Miss S. Jonas	837 R.S. Damerell	919 Dr M.S.H.	Turner
775 J. Kellaway	838 J.M. Mason	Chowdhury	977 Mrs Edith M. Turner
776	839 P.S. Goodmead	920 D.C. McGregor	978 Mr & Mrs P.H.
Mrs Oatway	840 A.F. Goodmead	921 H.D. Pengelly	U'ren
777	841 P. Photiou	922 R. Harding	979 Mr & Mrs C.C.
778 Ian Richardson	842 A. Wiseman	923 W.A.G. Jenkins	U'ren
779 L. Cresswell	843 Mrs N. Michael	924 E.J. Bird	980 Mrs C.P. Huddy
780 M.J. Moore	844 A.A. Wakley	925 V.L. Cluney	981 Miss D. Damerell
781 Mrs Ann Chiswell	845 E.A. Bailey	926 Dennis L. Ridgeway	982 Mr & Mrs D.W.
782 Mrs M. Ackland	846 Mrs P. Hamlyn	927 J. Vickery	Laver
783 Lawrence Ackland	847 K.G. Rogers	928 H.J. Lavers	983 Mrs J. Felmingham
784	848 P. Green	929 John A. Drew	984 Mrs S. Flower
P. Campbell	849 K.A. Froggatt	930 James Eric Hunt	985 Mrs F. Phipps
785	850 D. Mills	931 D.G.J. Burch	986 T. Bunker
786	851 W.J. Hookway	932 B.H. Emdon	987 Ranco Europe
Mrs B. Nicholls	852 Mrs C. Demuth	933 Lyn & Ian Wyatt	Limited
787	853 Mr & Mrs B. Bragg	934 Jay & John Thacker	996
788 G. Lewis	854 A. O'Sullivan	935 Mrs J.P. Bettison	997
789 A.G. Wilkin	855 M. Bridgeman	936 John Hooper	998 Plymouth College
790 M. Squires	856 Mrs A. Dockree	937 J. Eric Hunt FICS	999 Mrs J. Wheeler
791 R.W. Edwards	857 Mr & Mrs C. Palmer	938 Vanessa Jennifer	1000 Mrs M.M. Sings
792 Ms Stephanie E.	858 Derek G. Reynolds	Hunt	1001 Devon Library
Preece	859 John Blowey	939 Nigel E. Hunt	Services
793 J.P. King		940 The Librarian,	1083
794 Paul Hardwick		Plymouth College of	1084 Mrs J.L. Morris
795 D.R. Forshaw		Art & Design	
796 W.E. Chapman		941 R.G.E. York	*Remaining names unlisted*